I CAN
I WILL

Dynamics for
Personal Success

Always Remember I Can, I will!

Move forward with Confidence & determination

Sincerely,

FREDERICK G. ELIAS, Ph.D.

Frederick Elias

ODC Publishing
Santa Barbara/1992

This book is dedicated to all the people who were told they could not
accomplish what they set out to do and thought "I can't."
And through their persistence, they now say "I Can I Will!"

Second printing

Edited by Peter J. Elias, M.S.
Book design & typography by Jim Cook
Cover photo by David Roth
Cover design by Victoria Graphics
Printed by McNaughton & Gunn, Inc., Ann Arbor, Michigan.

Organizational Designs in Communication, Inc.
Post Office Box 60609
Santa Barbara, CA 93160

PUBLISHER'S CATALOGING IN PUBLICATION DATA
Elias, Frederick G., 1950-
    I can, I will: dynamics for personal success /
Frederick G. Elias.
        p.   cm.
    Includes bibliographical references
    ISBN: 1-881241-00-9
        1. Self-help techniques. 2. Success. 3. Life skills.
I. Title. II. Title: Dynamics for personal success.
BF632.E43   1992   158.1
                    QB192-10379

Contents

Opportunities for Change • The Relationship Between Beliefs and
Expectations • Self-Fulfilling Prophecy: Determining your
Destination • Self-Talk • Utilize Positive Self-Affirmations • Tune
In To Your Inner Self • Become More Dynamic • Climb More
Mountains

Motivate Yourself and Others • Active Listening • Make Good
Eye Contact to Show Interest • Observe Body Language and Take
In the Whole Picture When Listening • Seeing Versus Imagining •
Vocal Tone and Posture • Proactive Versus Reactive Responding •
Implicit Messages • Use the Power of Language • Use Your
Imagination as an Energy Source for Success and Fulfillment

Self-Imposed Detours and Barriers to Success • Fear of Success
Self-Judgement • Self-Guilt • Getting off Track • Thought
Stopping

Inner Barriers • Negative Preconceptions • Barriers of Fear •
Overcoming a False Self-Image • Integrating Your Self-Image •
Overcoming Toxic Relationships • Perseverance: The Key to
Overcoming Barriers • Planning Your Road Map to Personal
Success • A New Vista is a New Life • Shift Into Third Gear

Unexpressed Anger • Blaming Yourself or Blaming Others •
Giving Yourself or Others Mixed Messages • Failure to Accept
Reality and Realize Alternatives • Conditional Acceptance •
Overcoming Self-Sabotaging Behaviors

Getting Back on Track • Overcoming Resistance: The Key is
Optimism • Your Optimistic Self-Image • The Journey is More
Important Than the Destination • Self-Discipline and Focus

Never Say Fail!

Keep pushing—'tis wiser
    Than sitting aside,
And dreaming and sighing
    And waiting the tide.
In life's earnest battle
    They only prevail
Who daily march onward,
    And never say fail!

With an eye ever open—
    A tongue that's not dumb,
And a heart that will never
    To sorrow succumb—
You'll battle and conquer
    Though thousands assail:
How strong and how mighty,
    Who never say fail!

The spirit of angels
    Is active I know,
As higher and higher
    In glory they go:
Methinks on bright pinions
    From heaven they sail,
To cheer and encourage
    Who never say fail!

Ahead then keep pushing,
    And elbow your way,
Unheeding the envious,
    And asses that bray;
All obstacles vanish,
    All enemies quail,
In the might of their wisdom
    Who never say fail!

In life's rosy morning,
    In manhood's firm pride,
Let this be the motto
    Your footsteps to guide;
In storm and in sunshine,
    Whatever assail—
We'll onward and conquer,
    And never say fail!

ANONYMOUS

Foreword

Think about it: Your own destiny is either determined by yourself, or it is determined by chance. Another way of saying it is that when you drive your car, if you have a destination, you will get there. If you don't have a destination, you won't get anywhere. The "I Can I Will" Attitude puts you in the driver's seat on a direct route to the destination of your choice. This book is so powerful that you will almost immediately begin feeling in control of your destiny!

My friend, Dr. Fred Elias pulls from many sound systems of psychology; from encouragement to rational thinking and creates a synergy that will have you feeling turbo-charged in your drive through life. He inspires and teaches. His message is clear: "It's up to you. And you can do it!" The common sense ideas within will open roads to success, help you over, under, around and through the detours to your dreams, and create opportunities for change.

How much more will you get out of life if today you start taking an "I Can I Will" approach? This book is for you, or anyone you know who is ready to make their move on life's opportunities for change, and just needs a map. The young author shows you that your road to success is always under construction.

Get on the "Highway!" If you start reading this today rather than tomorrow, you'll get there a day sooner!

—Dr. Lewis E. Losoncy
Author of *The Encouragement Book*

Preface

"The difference between a successful person and others is not a lack of strength, not a lack of knowledge, but rather in a lack of will."

—Vince Lombardi

It was a cloudy day when I walked into the guidance counselor's office. This is the suggested course of action for graduating high school seniors before leaving the hallowed halls. The counselor barely looked at me when I walked in and sat down. He seemed more interested in the folder of papers resting on his wooden desk. After several seconds he glanced up half-heartedly and said, "Well, Frederick, what are your plans?" I replied hesitantly, "I want to go to college." His look was somber and his voice stern when he said, "You're not college material, you should go to a technical school and learn a trade."

"But I really want to go to college," I replied. My heart was beating rapidly. A feeling of panic and anxiety began to swell up inside of me. The feeling reminded me of the roaring sound of ocean waves beginning their downward plunge to the sandy beach and the rocks below. He was laughing at my new, exciting idea, and I was feeling the wind in my sails dying.

"I'm sorry," the guidance counselor replied, "You just won't make it, you're not college material." A feeling of anger and frustration emerged as I walked out of his office. On the verge of tears, I held back the flow with pride. I felt a warm current of electricity moving throughout my body as a sudden sense of urgency took over. I walked out of the front doors of that high school holding my head high and hearing a voice within me saying, "I Can I Will, I Can I Will!" This was my beginning—my turning point.

Acknowledgements

My sincere appreciation to my brother, Peter J. Elias, for his persever-ance, insight, and continuing dialogue.

A very special thanks to Lillian Elias, Susan Koller, Glenda Richter, Robert Hensley and Guy Rittger for their editorial excellence and suggestions.

Friends; Dr. Lewis Losoncy, Arnold Miller, and Harvey Mackay for their encouragement, Gordon Phelps for his beautiful illustrations, Tom Hansen and Karen Blum for their continual support, and Bill Lindert for his empowering messages.

I Can I Will

Choice and Decision Making went walking
down Haleakala, a volcanic crater with an
altitude of 10,000 feet, located on the island of
Maui, Hawaii. Half-way toward their
destination, Choice said to Decision Making,
"Will you continue on for the entire way?"

Decision Making replied, "There are many
paths with infinite possibilities. I will know
which decision to make when I get there."

Choice knew Decision Making to be wise,
and the two became one.

1.
Road to Success Under Construction

To see a world in a grain of sand,
And heaven in a wild flower;
Hold infinity in the palm of your hand,
And eternity in an hour.

—WILLIAM BLAKE

We are all unique as is the grain of sand in an infinite universe. When did you last experience your own uniqueness, your own individuality? It takes courage, and your own "*will*," to choose to be distinct from others. The first step is to realize that you are unique. Your ability to think, act, and feel in your own special way helps you to focus on, and crystallize, new opportunities for changing yourself. Your new changing self adapts to your changing environment. Beliefs about who you are, and what you aspire to become, create new avenues of opportunities and endless choices for self-improvement. Now is the time and opportunity to construct your personal road to success. Awaken yourself to experience the power of change that will consistently improve the quality of your life. Begin to experience the power of I Can I Will.

Opportunities for Change

Imagine being on a sailboat. The wind suddenly changes and the currents shift. What actions do you now take to adjust the sails and rudder to continue in your chosen direction? You cannot let the boat drift aimlessly lest you capsize. You must take action to set your new course. Human communication and interaction is like sailing. Changing the direction of your conversation, or intentions, is a matter of changing what you say, believe, and do. Once you are in control of your thoughts, feelings and actions, you can choose your own direction. Ultimately, you are in charge of the decisions and choices that you make. Keeping a balance, then, between intuition and rational thought and daring and caution allows you to harness energy and obtain peak performance, enabling you to master your perceptions and emotions. Face the wind and stand ready at the rudder.

When you begin to master your emotions and perceptions something unique happens. You increase your ability to communicate, changing the way you interact with others. Those around you may continue to behave the way they always have. You, however, have the 'free will' to change your emotional and physical reactions towards others. When you drive yourself to continually improve your relationships with others, your freedom of self-expression and self-confidence grows. *How* to accomplish these changes is discussed in detail in Chapter Two.

The way you view your world, and the way you interact with those around you, ultimately influences whether you change or choose not to change. When you give others the power to influence your response and reactions, you are allowing others to influence your behavior. You can control a situation by being in control of yourself. Only you can initiate the decision to change yourself. No one else can control your decisions, nor can you control anyone else's decisions, thoughts or reactions.

You are in charge of your own decisions and actions!

Seize the Day!

When you make a decision to change and take action, your self-image also changes. A change in your image requires a change in "awareness of self." Changing negative, discouraging experiences into positive, encouraging ones creates healthier thoughts and feelings. Healthy thoughts and feelings generate the mental and emotional resources needed for positive personal growth and success.

• **Realize that the way you think and feel defines the image you have of yourself.** Decide what *you* want for yourself. Positive changes allow you to embrace more of who you are and what you aspire to become. Seize all of your positive and enthusiastic feelings. Inspire and energize yourself!

• **Self-image transformation is a journey and a challenge.** Remember when you went on a vacation and changed your familiar scenery to something new and different? Wherever you travel, whether it be to see the redwood trees of California, to experience the brilliant colors of autumn in New England, to feel the warm waters in the South Pacific, or to contemplate the great architecture and art of Europe, when you return home you feel different, renewed. Conversations with others take on new meaning because of your new experiences. Time off, vacation, and recreation are essential for re-evaluation and self-growth.

When you experience changes within you, you begin to see yourself in a new light. The image you once had of yourself, comprised of your emotions, thoughts, beliefs and perceptions, is now changing. Internal change is based on changes in your self-image. Maxwell Maltz (1960) states in *Psycho-Cybernetics,*

> The self-image is the key to human personality and human behavior. Change the self-image and you change the personality and behavior. But more than this. The self-image sets the boundaries of individual accomplishment. It defines what you can and cannot be. Expand the self-image and you expand the area of the possible. The development of an adequately realistic self-image will seem to imbue the individual with new capabilities, new talents, and literally turn failure into success.

Change Your Self-image and You Change Your Attitude!

When you visualize yourself in a different way, your thoughts, feelings, and behaviors change accordingly. When you're willing to change, you empower yourself with the belief that reflects the feeling; *Yes—I Can I Will!*

Changing your self-image changes your attitude, behavior and communication with others. Deciding to use your time and energy to choose behaviors that will help you break out of unhealthy, destructive patterns facilitates personal growth. When you take action to develop healthy behaviors you empower yourself. Empowering yourself by taking control of and mastering your emotions and beliefs changes your self-image and behavior.

When you discipline and commit yourself to develop an attitude of self-confidence and determination, you take conscious control of your beliefs and actions. Consistently changing negative beliefs and actions into positive, productive ones moves you in the direction of strengthening your self-image. Your fresh vibrant attitude, communication, and self-image determine your success and will turn your dreams into reality.

Now is the time to use your imagination as an energy source for success and fulfillment. Imagine yourself:

- free from unreasonable guilt and fear
- overcoming limiting beliefs and emotions
- being spontaneous
- thinking in a nonjudgmental way
- accomplishing all your personal goals
- feeling self-confident and self-determined
- enjoying your work and life
- taking part in an adventure
- harnessing your inner power to overcome any obstacle
- climbing more mountains
- becoming more dynamic

Create the life you envision for yourself. Realize that when you become committed to achieving all that you desire, you set the stage for lifelong growth and self-awareness. Decide what you want and clarify how you *can* and *will* achieve your goals—your deepest desires. Challenge yourself, and take action now! Change your self-image and determine your personal success and direction in life!

The Relationship Between Beliefs and Expectations

Your beliefs and expectations play an important role in understanding your personal development. How many times have you attempted to change yourself, or your situation, without truly believing or expecting that your goal would be achieved? When you develop positive beliefs and expectations you will be more successful in accomplishing your goals.

The first step in the process of developing personal success is to remember to *actively train yourself to change your negative behaviors into positive ones.* The second step is to *discipline yourself and focus on developing a positive, mental attitude.* A positive attitude and high expectations significantly determine your performance and achievement. To change your behavior and your attitude:

> You have to believe that you can and will,
> and take action to do so.

You are the facilitator of your own change process. When you realize that you have the power to change your behavior and your attitude, you empower yourself to make the right decisions. Taking action, and deciding to develop your plan for personal success, will change your beliefs, your attitude and your self-image.

Developing a positive attitude, becoming more self-acceptant, and communicating more effectively with others, help you develop your inner resources of optimism and understanding. Begin to see yourself as a person who's fully capable of making meaningful choices in your life. Remember, your potential is unlimited. Developing and achieving your goals for personal success depends on the positive changes you make in your life. Ultimately, you decide how successful you'll become in your personal and professional relationships. Become a winner. Winners know that to get what you expect in life an attitude of positive self-control is essential. Winners would say, "I was good today, and I'll be better tomorrow." Speak up for what you believe is right, and know you deserve and intend to get the same rights as others. Top performance demands energy, effort, and a willingness to put up with frustrations.

As a winner, your personal sacrifice, hard work, and inner strength and courage motivates you to believe: I *can* achieve. Believing you can achieve will activate your courage and enthusiasm to become responsible for your purpose and goals. The most important proof of *"believing you can achieve"* involves changes in your beliefs and actions. When you believe you can achieve, the next step is to choose new beliefs and behaviors. These new beliefs and behaviors will move you in the direction of discovering what triggers positive emotions. Positive beliefs and emotions encourage you to expect more and become more active and involved with your plans and goals.

Charles Garfield (1984) believes that achieving peak performance begins with the "discovery of complete acceptance, and development of skills to exercise consciously the power of volition (will). This power makes itself known in a variety of ways, as an all encompassing desire for success, or in the feeling, 'I will do it', or simply making the commitment to accomplish something that is particularly important to you" (p. 33). Your inner belief and motivation creates the power within you to accomplish your goals, plans, and dreams.

Focus on becoming the person with "a desire to succeed." You can do it! Your transformation and movement forward is embedded in the belief: I Can I Will.

Self-Fulfilling Prophecy: Determining Your Destination

Your self-concept is determined by the perceptions you have of yourself—the way you see yourself. Your beliefs and expectations about who you are and how you fit into various situations plays an important role in the formation of your attitude and your self-image. Beliefs and expectations from others about who you are and what you can or cannot accomplish also contributes to changes in your self-image. Beliefs can either lubricate your success or create friction to halt positive changes in your achievement.

In *Think Your Way to Success* Lewis Losoncy (1982) writes, "Your success is preceded by the belief that you can succeed" (p. 34). A student's attitude about himself and his abilities plays a primary role in how he performs in school. Some educators continue to give students remedial training when what pupils really need is an altered and positive vision that reflects a belief, "I can and will learn." It's not just your ability or competency in a certain subject, but it's also your beliefs and expectations about yourself that will determine whether or not you will succeed.

By focusing on creating positive beliefs, and taking positive action, you'll yield positive results. On the other hand, creating negative beliefs, and taking negative action, yields negative results. When you create a self-image of inadequacy and failure, you build the negative reality and reinforce your own failure. You get caught up in your own failure script and become predetermined to fail in everything you attempt. When you believe you'll fail, a self-fulfilling prophecy of failure emerges. Rather than experiencing the fruits of success, you allow yourself to give in to your self-defeating beliefs. If you believe you can't change things, your self-image will work overtime making sure that you don't succeed.

Ultimately, your beliefs determine your self-esteem and your success. The higher your self-esteem, the greater will be your self-confidence and the ability to handle yourself positively in various situations. Beliefs and expectations from others also influence and determine how you define yourself, and the actions you eventually take. When a person you value highly believes in you, their beliefs and actions influence you to believe in yourself, increasing your self-esteem.

Positively reinforce the beliefs, behaviors and desires that will help you, and others, achieve success. Your positive beliefs and perceptions paint a bright picture of reality, increasing your optimism and motivation.

Self-Talk

Decide to improve the way you view life. A positive change in your perspective will change your self-image and self-esteem. One way to change your perspective is by developing positive self-talk. Positive self-talk utilizes your own inner voice. Your ability to control and consistently use positive self-talk boosts self-confidence. It's important to change negative thoughts and emotions into positive beliefs about what you *can* and *will* do. As you continue to channel your thoughts and ideas in a positive and healthy way, you begin to overcome negative thoughts and beliefs.

One way to re-program your negative thoughts into positive ones is to mentally recite, ''I am determined to reach my goal, I am concentrating on my success.'' How successful you become is determined by your motivation and positive beliefs about yourself. You bolster your self-confidence and empower yourself when you willingly choose your own thoughts and beliefs.

Do you allow others to set goals that overwhelm you and leave you with feelings of doubt and fear, especially when you fail to reach them? When someone else continually sets goals for you, your sense of self-esteem is diminished. You increase your probability of following through on a task when you set the goal yourself.

When you set a goal do not allow others to restrict you by telling you that your goal is unrealistic. You have a choice. You can let their limited vision persuade you by telling yourself that they're right or, you can persuade yourself by using positive self-talk that will help you concentrate on fulfilling your goal. Utilizing positive self-talk will prepare you for taking the necessary steps to make your goals a reality.

Changing your self-talk to clearly define, and crystallize, your goals and desires is the first step toward attaining them. Then, breaking up your goals and desires into manageable parts helps you to see what additional steps need to be taken to get the results you need. Initially, setting your sights to achieve a moderate amount of success is the best way to reach your goals. To reach your goal, move forward and develop a realistic plan to achieve immediate success. This will help you overcome overwhelming feelings of doubt and fear. As you complete each objective celebrate your success along the way.

Taking action to change your self-talk changes your self-image, awakening your awareness. What you tell yourself affects your emotional life. When your emotional life is affected, your mental and physical life are affected as well. This highly interactive and reciprocal condition forms the basis for all personal, behavioral and motivational change.

Changing your self-image will create a change in what you do and how you do it. A positive change in your self-image is a powerful asset to help you create success in your life. Experiencing a positive change in your self-image raises your self-esteem. Your heightened sense of self-esteem allows you to appreciate yourself for who you are and the qualities you possess.

I can and I will change my future.
I can and I will change my life.

When you change your self-image, you change your life. What an exhilarating thought!

Changing your self-image also has an effect on others. Once you begin to see and experience changes in your life, you will ultimately help others to change. Showing concern, and expressing yourself in positive ways, can change the other person's sense of him/herself. You have a choice. You can either encourage or discourage the beliefs of others.

Encouraging others will change the image they have of themselves. By changing your self-image and increasing your self-esteem, you will help others to increase their self-esteem as well. In a reciprocal relationship, when you respond favorably to someone, or express yourself positively, most of the time the response that is returned will be a positive one. When you change your self-image, others will believe that they can change their self-image.

Life takes on new meaning when you instill a sense of self-worth and pride in yourself and in others. The drive for self-worth is a universal motivation among humans. It's important to be aware of the kinds of relationships and situations which help to build your sense of self-worth, and those which diminish your sense of self-worth.

Accepting new challenges helps you to use your energies to achieve whatever you set out to accomplish. Pay attention to the *how* and *what* you communicate, verbally and nonverbally. Use all of your inner and outer resources to project a strong, positive self-image. Accent your positive inner and outer characteristics. Choose to expand your boundaries and accomplish more. Set yourself up for success by becoming a winner, and an achiever. When you become a successful, encouraging human being, you'll find your way and help others find their way. Helping and encouraging others is to become a self-esteem enhancer.

Have faith in yourself. When you have faith, you will move mountains that seemed immovable and realize dreams that seemed unreachable. Developing your positive beliefs creates choices for successful outcomes. Identify with the conditions, or situations, that generate positive feelings and self-worth. Don't leave things to chance. Having faith is not a vague, or unclear, proposition. It means that your beliefs are based on rational thought, accurate information and empowering actions.

When you perceive what you need with accuracy, you'll be more congruent and successful in reaching your goals. Don't throw your life's decisions into someone else's hands. Create a compelling future for yourself by taking responsibility for life's challenges. Have faith in your ability to make your own decisions! Your willingness to take risks and experience new situations is a measure of your faith. Encourage others to rely less on hope and more on themselves. Acknowledge your innovative spirit and guide your feelings, thoughts and actions in the directions that you choose.

Use Positive Self-Affirmations

Positive self-affirmations are powerful tools to help you overcome negative beliefs and emotions. Nonjudgmental positive affirmations help you feel good about yourself while making the transition from being discouraged to becoming more encouraged. Becoming more encouraged motivates you to eliminate negative thoughts and take positive action.

My friend Robert tried to convince me to verbally recite self-affirmations. He said the process would help me change my life. In the beginning, I was sceptical. I took his advice and made a list of ten, positive self-affirmations and read them out loud every morning and evening.

As time passed, I began to feel, see, hear, and experience the effects that the positive self-affirmations were having on me. I became more positive and accepting of new ideas without judging them, or myself. This freedom from judgement allowed me to dismiss my negative thoughts, and become more open to opportunities for positive change in my life. Once my beliefs and thoughts changed, I began taking more positive action.

Self-affirmative statements are an easy first step. When you actively and assertively make a conscious commitment to recite self-affirmations on a continual basis, you will begin to overcome negative beliefs and emotions. When you begin to adopt positive self-affirmations as a building block to reaching your full potential, it is important to choose goals that can be achieved in a relatively short time. Initial successes will help you energize your self-image and beliefs. Your daily success will lead to the final product and help you achieve the results you desire.

Powerful self-affirmations have helped me change my beliefs and emotional states. When you commit yourself by verbally reciting affirmations on a continual basis, you'll change your mental and emotional state. Examples of positive self-affirmations that will assist you in turning negatives into positives are as follows:

- I am successful in my communication with others.
- I have total financial and emotional support in all my work.

- I am supportive of others.
- My natural affinities bring me the right relationships with the right people for a prosperous and meaningful life.
- I am open and aware of new information that provides me with life-giving experiences.
- Peace and intelligence are shining through me in my interactions with others.
- Today is filled with excellence, happiness and prosperity.
- I am taking action to create a life filled with passion.
- I am free from unreasonable guilt and conditioning which no longer serves me.
- I become stronger as I condition myself for success.

What other examples of positive self-affirmations can you think of that will help your strategy for becoming a risk-taker and a momentum-maker?

_____

_____

_____

Practicing positive affirmations will grant you freedom from unreasonable guilt and fear, and help you overcome limiting beliefs and emotions. Positively changing yourself, physically and emotionally, will facilitate a change in your identity. If you experience a discouraging inner voice that emerges when you are attempting to state a positive affirmation, explore the origin of the voice.

Sometimes discouraging inner voices are messages that we have internalized from often well meaning parents or other authority figures. Although these voices may have been appropriate in past situations, they can now prevent us from achieving our full potential. The new voice, or positive affirmation, allows new opportunities to come forward that will make life brighter and more joyful.

Changing the way you think will change the way you act. Making positive changes in the way you act facilitates the belief that your actions will lead to positive life changes. When you develop positive life changes, you create opportunities to eliminate unreasonable guilt and fear from your life. This opportunity and newfound freedom empowers you to overcome your limiting beliefs and emotions.

Change your limiting beliefs and emotions and create the success you deserve. Awaken your inner courage and take the first step by consciously creating and reciting your positive self-affirmations. Make those changes that will lead to more effective long-range goal attainment while promoting your ultimate health and vitality.

Tune In to Your Inner Self

Become more self-confident and self-determined. When you want to make positive life changes, stop living and experiencing life from the rearview mirror. Move your eyes to the front windshield and put your hands on the steering wheel. Becoming more self-confident and self-determined means you've decided to change your life in a positive way. When you start tuning-in to your inner self, the positive changes you've made in your beliefs and behaviors begin to eliminate unhealthy thoughts and actions. The excitement of tuning-in to yourself and discovering your hidden or untapped potential is like embarking on a journey to explore a new world. William James said, ''Only humans have the power to change their outer world by the change in their inner world.''

Tuning-in to your inner world of thoughts and feelings, and your outer world of sensory perceptions (touch, taste, smell, sight and sound), is a journey of growth and awareness. Using your mind and senses to understand yourself, and make connections with others, is like turning the dial or pushing the button to adjust the wavelength on your stereo receiver. After selecting the channel you want, it's then just a matter of adjusting the volume.

First, you are a signal source similar to that of a radio transmitter. And second, you are a receiver similar to that of a radio receiver.

As a transmitter, you send out a variety of verbal and nonverbal signals. Sometimes these signals conflict with each other. When you're able to control your outgoing signals and put them to good use, you can emphasize what you're attempting to communicate. It is important that as transmitters of information your outgoing signals are communicated in a direct and clear manner. *How* you communicate is just as important as *what* you communicate.

As receivers, you can tune-in to different incoming signals. Just like the FM receiver you have at home, tuning-in to one station at a time is easier than trying to listen to two or three at the same time.

Once you tune-in to the signal, you will receive clear messages and sounds from your system. Once you are tuned-in, and the sound is clear, you can also increase or decrease the volume. Monitoring your stereo's volume is similar to adjusting the input and messages you receive from others. Monitoring volume is important when you're learning to listen to yourself, and to others. It's difficult to hear what another person is saying if you are continually talking.

When you want to truly hear others you must decrease your own communication. Listening requires that you tune down your own volume and turn up your empathy and compassion—the language of the heart.

The language of the heart is a silent communication in which you convey empathy, warmth, and understanding to others. You hear with your entire body through your senses. When you hear what others are saying, verbally and nonverbally, your response is more accurate and precise. Receiving clear messages, then, from others ultimately depends on the extent that you listen and send clear communications.

When you take responsibility for your conversations, you build trust and self-confidence within yourself, and in others. Remember, one way to create long-lasting joy and spontaneity in your communications is to listen and respond with sincerity.

Experience a Joy Ride

Imagine being in your car and driving with no goal or final destination in mind. How do you get to where you're going? Do you let others around you determine your final destination? How can you realize your full potential, and be all that you can become, if you are always listening to backseat drivers?

When you are driving you have to be totally present and aware of other vehicles, traffic signals, pedestrians, and your actions or reactions in various situations. Backseat drivers only see part of the picture. They try to conceptualize what they see from a limited perspective and with limited vision. As the driver, you're spontaneously sensing every movement of your vehicle as well as the movement of other vehicles. *Depend on your vision.* The direction you take is your decision. Besides, enjoy the ride. Enjoying the journey while getting to your destination is equally important and fulfilling.

Driving is similar to living life. Ideally, you're paying attention to the here-and-now rather than living in the past. Are you living life from the backseat? Are you content getting to your destination by letting someone else drive you? Or do you arrive at your destination by taking the wheel into your own hands?

When you are driving you focus on where you are headed, not where you have been. Living in a mechanized way and focusing on your past experiences loses all the spontaneity and fun of being in the present. Life is to be lived within all its splendor and beauty, not traded or conceptualized and squeezed into a pattern of systems. Taking a new route can be challenging and exciting.

Dedicate your life to developing your full potential. Become who you are and don't settle for what you think you 'should' be like. When you attempt to actualize a concept of what you should be like, rather than to actualize your true self, you only become discouraged. As the driver, you're in control of where you're going. You decide which turns to make for healthier and happier outcomes.

When you decide to go on vacation with your companion, or with a friend, do you discuss the endless possibilities of where you want to go, and then spend the next several hours deciding on how you're going to get there? Endless debates and options takes all the fun out of the journey. Getting caught up in the menu of choices and fruitless debates only leaves you frustrated and further away from your decision. Maybe you're content with saying, ''I'll wait until my decision comes to me.'' Chances are you'll be waiting for a long time.

Once you've made your decision, getting to your destination, both physically and emotionally, requires that you create healthy habits and patterns to power you toward your goals. Realizing your potential means making a commitment to understand your inner motivations, your inner image, and your goals. Getting to know yourself and understanding your motivations are similar to reading a map. A map is an image of a territory that tells you where to go and what direction to take to reach your desired destination. Understanding your behaviors, the ones that pull you further away from and the ones that move you closer to your goals, is essential for successfully getting to your destination. Make the journey educational and joyful.

The only way you will not get to your destination is if you stop. If you spend too much energy 'imagining' how you'll get to your destination without actually doing something about it, you'll probably be in the exact same place as you were a moment ago. A map, or plan, is the most effective tool in helping you reach your destination.

For example, when you want to get physically and mentally fit, you *must* decide *how* you want to achieve these goals. Planning to get regular exercise, choosing a healthy diet, avoiding undue mental stress and worry, and actively seeking out new challenges and learning experiences that stimulate your mind, will help you strengthen your commitment to achieving these goals. Create your plan and go for it! When you know where you're headed move in that direction. Whether your destination be discovering who you are, or where you want to go, enjoy the experience. Increasing the quality of your decisions *can* and *will* move you in the direction of your dreams!

Positive Self-Imaging is a constructive approach to help you get to your destination. The practice of mental imaging gives you a psychological map to your unconscious and conscious behaviors. When you mentally focus on where it is you want to go, and you're committed to reaching your destination, your actions usually follow. Dr. Wayne Dyer (1989) is right when he asserts that your "actions come from your images." That is, you usually won't act if you haven't already seen yourself mentally rehearsing the situation. How you visually depict yourself, in any given situation, is what you will become, and how you will act. When you reinforce your images in a positive way, positive things happen. Focusing on making positive, pleasurable changes in your life reinforces you with uplifting feelings of self-confidence and self-determination.

Imagine yourself walking down a path across a field and coming to a barbed-wire fence. If you see the fence as an insurmountable barrier toward completing your goal, then the barrier will remain. When you see the fence as having a gate in it, or when you find a way of going over, around or through it, then the fence is merely one more obstacle to overcome. Nothing more, nothing less.

When you give too much power to any obstacle, or person, you automatically place yourself in a no-win situation. One way to overcome this no-win situation is to change the rules. See the situation as an opportunity, or challenge, to use your imagination—your mind. When the situation is no longer challenging or healthy, and you're using too much energy with few results, choose a new direction where there will be new challenges and opportunities. There's no reason to set yourself up for failure or punishment. Deciding to create positive beliefs and expectations about yourself influences the actions you take.

You can change your situation by focusing on making moderate changes and giving careful thought to your long-term goals. A goal to complete a degree from a four-year college within six years is not unrealistic. Don't expect to do it in two and set yourself up for failure. Choose a plan you can realistically follow. Emotional, physical, and mental plateaus and peaks are normal experiences on the road to success. Focusing on your progress and remembering where you started creates confidence and courage. Improving yourself, and your life, requires concentration and self-discipline. Appreciate the journey. When you apply yourself, you will do it!

Believe in Yourself—Know Where You're Going

When you believe in yourself, you feel capable of encouraging yourself and others, professionally and personally. Your attitude and self-esteem reach new heights. High self-esteem and a positive self-image help you overcome problems that may otherwise overwhelm you. Belief in yourself will ultimately result in having others believe in you. When you have a direction, and know where you are going, you will increase your ability to perform a particular task. When you have social and emotional support from others, you're more hopeful and experience less stress. You also have an amazing ability to cope with the damaging effects of negative or condemning statements from others. Hope and self-esteem are the medicine that transforms a negative self-image into a positive one.

Failure is the result of acknowledging disbelief in yourself.

One way to increase your motivation, and stop your self-sabotaging beliefs, is to give yourself permission to get what you need. Right Now! This may be a financial, social, psychological or physical reward. Demotivation is the result of persistent procrastination, or believing you don't have a future.

First, admit that you may have to make changes in an uncomfortable or unhealthy situation. Lifestyle and relationship changes are sometimes the most difficult ones to make. Second, realize that you are a constantly changing person. You can change your ideas about the world, about people, and about who you are. You will not be the same tomorrow as you are today. And you will not be the same next week as you are tomorrow. Believe that you have a future and start living it— right now!

Harness Your Power Within To Overcome Any Obstacle

When you believe in yourself, you become more encouraged and more enthusiastic. Expressing positive emotions and ideas to others allows you to present an image of success, breaking self-limiting patterns in your past behavior. The way to harness your inner power and get started on developing your personal success is to experience your future success in the present. Continually encourage yourself to speak positively about who you are and where you're going, personally and professionally.

When I first began my consulting practice, after completing my Doctorate degree in Education, funds were low, and everyone kept telling me how difficult it was starting a new business. What they did not include in their dismal forecast was all the knowledge and information that I would gain by meeting new people and working in different companies, both business and academic. Every sunrise after drinking my juice and coffee, and feeling the early morning sun, I read this quote from Goethe:

Until one is committed there is hesitancy, the chance to draw back, always ineffective, concerning all acts of initiative (and creation). There is one elementary truth, the ignorance of which kills countless ideas and splendid plans: that the moment one definitely commits oneself, then providence moves too. All sorts of things occur to help one that would never otherwise have occurred. A whole stream of events issues from the decision, raising in one's favor all manner of unforeseen incidents and meetings and material assistance which no man could have dreamed would have come his way. Whatever you can do, or dream you can, begin it. Boldness has genius, power and magic in it. Begin it now.

As my commitment grew, my course was set and success began. The power created in affirming your individuality—your identity and sense of 'self'- is immense. When you feel empowered your sense of self-worth increases and your self-concept changes. Struggling to build and protect your self-esteem is an ongoing human process and motivation. Positive changes in your self-esteem and self-worth motivate and drive you to become more committed to yourself, your goals, and your aspirations. Maxwell Maltz (1960) asserts, "Of all the traps and pitfalls in life, self-disesteem is the deadliest, and the hardest to overcome; for it is a pit designed and dug by our own hands."

Was there a time when you said, "I probably won't pass this test." Or, "I'll never be any good at sports, others will have to make up for my inadequacies." How about this one, "I've failed in relationships before, there's no use in trying to make this one work." These statements are examples of self-disesteem. This is the time when you need support from others and a dream you can believe in. "If one advances confidently in the direction of his dream, and endeavors to live the life which he has imagined, he will meet with a success unexpected in common hours," stated Henry David Thoreau.

The ultimate dream is to believe in yourself more than you have ever imagined. When you learn that you control what you choose to feel, think and say, you'll be on a road where there are no bypaths leading to self-disesteem and discouragement. You *can* and *will* overcome any obstacle when you advance confidently in the direction of your dreams.

Become More Dynamic

When was the last time you tried something new and exciting like—a trip to a tropical island . . . a windjammer cruise . . . skiing in the Alps or Colorado . . . a hot air balloon ride . . . test driving a high-powered sports car . . . snorkeling in Hawaii's Molokini Bay, an island created from a volcanic crater . . . experiencing an outward bound/ropes course . . . or looking deep within yourself to search and find your destiny?

When you decide on a new resolution, has your inner voice ever said, "What does it matter if I . . . go for a walk around the block . . . take a run on the beach . . . start an exercise or weight reduction program . . . try a new hairstyle, or wear vibrantly colored new clothes."

Becoming more dynamic requires inner focus and drive. It also means overcoming negative self-talk. Accepting and experiencing your small changes—your small wins—one at a time is essential to reinforce your behavior to change and become successful.

Create effective strategies to experience immediate and consistent success. When you start exercising, for example, the first thing you do is learn how to stretch your muscles. Just as basketball and baseball players warm-up before the game, you must also warm-up and stretch, and ride the stationary bike for several minutes. As you stretch, you begin to relax your mental state. Your mental and emotional states must be in harmony with your physical state before you even touch a barbell, or use the machinery. And when you begin lifting weights, you start out with 10 lbs. or 20 lbs., not 100 lbs. immediately. As you condition yourself physically, you condition yourself mentally. Allow yourself that special feeling of appreciation and recognition once you've accomplished small wins in your effort to become more dynamic. Enjoy your success and remain in the present moment as you continue on with your workout.

After several weeks of physical conditioning and when you're warmed-up and ready, that is, when your inner focus is in line with your mental stamina and physical drive, go for the big wins. You're now prepared to take the big risks because you've already built up your mental conditioning by initially taking small steps. When your drive comes from within, you gain the ability, and power, to change your mental and emotional states. Like the fine-tuned body of an athlete, you are mentally and emotionally conditioned for success.

Once you maintain your inner focus and drive, you change your mental, emotional, and physical condition. You are then able to successfully let go of anxiety, fear of failure, and old habits that divert your attention from being in the present moment, the here-and-now. Eliminating your fear of failure will increase your confidence and ability to use your mental faculties in a positive way. One positive way is to focus your attention on the present. This will create a unity between mind and body, a dynamic energy that produces a feeling of confidence and optimism. Another way is to take personal responsibility for your actions, rather than leaving them to chance. Taking personal responsibility for your actions helps you make positive changes in your attitude and feelings. This highly energized state, or awareness, gets you in touch with your whole body and its movements, and the movements of others.

This is best exemplified when you are playing a team sport. Your own personal drive, enthusiasm and momentum, help you and other team members focus on the goal. For example, during a volleyball game, when you're totally in the moment, you're focused on what's going on and can predict where the other person is going to hit the ball. You can predict, by body motion, where the next action will take place. Everything stops. You don't hear the crowd. You don't hear yourself breathing. The only movement is the action of the volleyball. And it's your responsibility to be responsive to yourself.

When you are responsible for yourself the whole team benefits. When you're responsible and recognize that your emotions, decisions and behaviors are created within you, your energies become focused in the direction where success is inevitable. The positive ways you see yourself are the building blocks of self-esteem. When you see yourself in a positive way, you then begin to act on these beliefs. This allows you to grow and take responsibility for your actions. When you take responsibility for your life, you become responsible for everything you feel, think and do. Once you begin to feel and accept your new, positive feelings, you can choose to act in more positive and self-directed ways. Depending on yourself and becoming self-reliant empowers you to believe in yourself and become the person you desire. When you change your attitude, you begin to discover new meaning in your life.

> Only you have control over what you want to become
> and what you want to accomplish.

Success is not solely determined by the accumulation of money or material things, rather it is the opportunity to participate in life at a more meaningful level. One must experience feelings of both accomplishment and meaning in their work to be truly successful. The greatest artist in the world does not need an audience to express him/herself. History is filled with examples of great artists who went unrecognized during their lifetime and suffered in poverty through life fighting discouragement—yet they were persistent in their endeavors. Real success is when your efforts and accomplishments attain meaning for yourself and are shared by others. Expressing your highest aspirations by connecting and communicating with others brings greater meaning to your accomplishments. This is self-encouraging as well as encouraging to others.

Designing and planning your life to become successful is a continuous process. You can learn from the trials and tribulations from the lives of past role models; however, focus on your own vision and path. Develop your own point of view.

Your success depends on integrating your mental and emotional states to create a positive change in how you feel and what you do. Ultimately, you are in charge of the changes taking place in your life. When you change the way you act, you change the way you feel about yourself. When you change the way you feel and act, you will change your relations with others. This harmony and balance created between your emotional, mental and physical states creates a synergy that will fill your life with greater meaning and self-understanding.

Synergy, a cooperative process integrating your mental, emotional, physical and spiritual states, or conditions, creates an energy to foster the healthy development of your self-image. When you unify these states, you will have a better understanding of yourself and increase your ability to understand and relate to others more effectively. Integrating your self-image will bring greater self-understanding. Developing meaningful interactions with others, and choosing healthy behaviors based on your sound decisions, will empower, influence and change your life.

Your personal success depends on you! Now is the time to begin acting with conviction and become more focused. Drive yourself to make the positive changes in your attitude and watch your self-respect and motivation soar. As Bertrand Russell said, "In the vast realm of the human mind there are no limitations."

Your desire to expand your mind and condition your body will lift your self-esteem and confidence. As you build yourself into one powerful human being, you begin to find the harmony and congruence between your emotions, beliefs and actions. Run the race with the firm conviction that you *will* achieve your goals. Keep your enthusiasm high and become a more successful, dynamic you!

Climb More Mountains

You can lift yourself out of a meaningless life and create the breakthrough you deserve. You have the ability and power to change your self-image, therefore yourself. It's time to start moving in the direction of your dreams. There is no evidence that you will fail. Choosing the path of success is the first decision you must make to loosen the shackles of your past failures. As Harvey Mackay (1990) puts it,

"Measure success by success, not by the number of failures it takes to achieve it."

The second step is looking in the mirror with a firm conviction and belief in yourself. Look in the mirror of life and see the resources available to you to accomplish your goals. Using your resources to make powerful decisions strengthens your commitment to achieve success. Learning to climb a mountain is similar to learning how to become successful. You must plant each foot firmly and maintain focus before taking the next step.

Learning is not only the accumulation of knowledge, it is the application of knowledge. Learning is a movement from moment to moment. Learning by its nature requires that you remain flexible in your thinking, maintaining an openness to change. *Believing* you can create your own destiny is the first step. The second step is *willing* yourself to take the necessary action to effect your destiny.

Focus your knowledge and energy on developing the positive relationships you deserve. Focus your strengths, assets, and resources to discover the possibilities of life that are congruent with the realization of your highest potential. Your consciousness is like the butterfly emerging from the metamorphosis of the cocoon, a new cycle of life begins.

Be all that you can, and that you will. All it takes each day is just one more try, one more opportunity to change your self-image. The Dynamics for Personal Success are continually regenerating within you.

Empower yourself—NOW!

2.
Communication Skills for Growth

Have you ever wondered why some people are highly motivated and successful in everything they set out to accomplish, while others, who may come from similar backgrounds, fail? What gives some the edge and pushes them to the top, while others have a difficult time getting motivated to move forward? The most important difference between being motivated or demotivated is attitude. A positive attitude and positive self-image create the difference between success and failure in every facet of your existence. Attitude, motivation, and communication skills are the cornerstones for growth. They provide the foundation for success in meeting any challenge.

Motivate Yourself and Others

Motivation is a lifelong process—a process by which you become renewed each and every day. The eminent Scandinavian philosopher, Søren Kierkegaard, believed that an individual is constantly in the process of becoming . . . and translates all his thinking into terms of process. To motivate yourself and others, you must first learn to recognize the process by which you create negative communication and demotivating behaviors. Acknowledging your negative communications is often the first step toward changing them. Learning the skills to change patterns of behavior that inhibit you enables you to continue in your process of growth.

When you believe you are discouraged, you are simultaneously reinforcing your discouraging beliefs and behavior. If you believe you can't do something, your beliefs and behavior will make you unsuccessful. However, when you take the first step to change the phrase "I can't" to "I won't," you become more responsible for your actions and beliefs. By taking this responsibility you become more self-accepting. You can now communicate with more confidence. Communicating with confidence positively changes the way you feel and act toward others. You can motivate and boost the confidence of others when you feel personally confident and motivated. Give yourself permission to make the courageous changes that will motivate you to take positive action. Focus your energies in the direction where you create encouraging beliefs and behavior, and you will be successful.

The second step is changing the "I won't" to "I can." Taking this action helps you develop even more responsibility for your decisions. You are now in charge of making your own decisions, and can now decide what it is you want to accomplish. The "I can" is an important step in the motivation process. You look less for approval or disapproval from others, knowing that your choice comes from within you. Charles Garfield wrote, "As a peak performer, you will know that your triumphs come about not because luck favored you but because of the active responsibility you have taken." When you take the action necessary to change "I won't" to "I can," you become more focused and self-determined.

The "I Can" is a movement forward in communication. It helps you realize that you can make your own decisions and create your own behavior. The "I Can" creates success because it motivates you to make positive changes in your beliefs, communication and behavior. Changing the "I Can" to "I Will" creates a dynamic change in your life, the transition from what is potential to what is actual. "I Can" is the spark that ignites your fire. "I Will" is your inner fire and torch that motivate you to take action. Taking action can be difficult, but is also challenging, exciting and rewarding. "I Will" is your inner determination, driving force and motivation to choose and focus on maximizing your abilities. Invoking "I Can I Will" is to call on your inner strength for encouragement, inspiration, and support. "I Can I Will" focuses and drives you to move forward with greater momentum.

Motivate yourself and others by effectively choosing to practice the skills for growth which contribute to success. Maximizing your abilities, or "going for the gold," in sports, education, business, medicine, or any other field of endeavor, means having the courage to "take a chance" and try something new. Choose to take action and live dynamically. Practice the mechanics and skills for growth. Take the initial first step to change your behavior and fine-tune your communications.

Active Listening

Your commitment to interact and make good contact with others requires focus and concentration. Refrain from monopolizing the conversation. Remember, listening to others is as important as communicating. Sharing ideas and information allows others the freedom to make their own decisions. Helping to generate alternatives is not the same as giving advice. When you give advice, you take away (sometimes unintentionally) the person's freedom to make his or her own choice. You can only communicate accurately when you have heard what others have to say.

Communicating honestly with yourself leads to personal growth and understanding. When your communication is understood, you feel accepted. However, refusing to listen to yourself or others creates confusion and misunderstandings. When communication is one-way, making contact with others is rarely successful because you're so concerned with the importance of your own message that you fail to listen. Imagine two rails of a train track being six feet apart from one another. You are riding on one rail and your friend is on another. The rails, however, never intersect. Parallel communication, or collective monologue, occurs when the discussion between two people never intersects. The conversation might sound something like this:

Speaker One: I had a flat tire last night while travelling home from my business meeting. I got upset.

Speaker Two: Oh, I had a flat tire when I was coming home from a meeting, I really got upset.

Speaker One: And to top it all off, my spare was flat and I had to walk 10 miles to the nearest station.

Speaker Two: My spare was flat and I walked at least 10 miles to the station.

Parallel communication reduces the possibility for two people to connect in a meaningful way and develop empathy. It is one-way and can often frustrate one or both speakers.

Successful communication is two-way. The rails of the train track intersect. Two-way or active listening involves a speaker and a listener. While one person is speaking, the listener is reflecting on the meaning—the emotional content—of the speaker's message. There is a mutual acceptance and recognition that "it takes two" to make true communication happen.

When you understand the other person's intentions, you can empathize without jumping to conclusions. Facilitating communication, together with helping others overcome barriers that prevent their effective communication, is an opportunity to understand what the other person really means. When you learn to listen to others, you become more effective in your interpersonal communication and relationships. Developing sensitive communications helps you become more successful. It also reduces the risk of alienating others before you've had a chance to know what they really mean.

Basic, positive communications, both verbal and nonverbal, are fundamental to active listening. For example, nonverbal cues such as head nods, leaning forward, and a slight tilt of the head all indicate active listening. Simple verbal responses (such as "Of course," "I understand"), repetition of key words, and restatement of key phrases encourage the speaker to continue talking. By actively listening, you're acting as a facilitator for the speaker while engaging in meaningful conversation.

Repetition of key words and restating key phrases is shown in the following examples. As the active listener, repeating key words in the speaker's message means you *choose* one word that you think best represents what he is feeling.

Student: I'm really having trouble with this instructor.
Listener: Trouble?
Student: She really irritates me.
Listener: Irritates you?

By restating key words, the listener shows interest. The speaker will probably continue on with the conversation.

Restating key *phrases* is the next step the listener takes which helps the speaker focus on what he/she means.

Student:	Yes, I can't figure her out. I never know what she's thinking. She's always changing the rules.
Listener:	Changing the rules? (with a slight nod of the head).
Student:	Right! Changing the rules. She says one thing but expects something totally different.

Restating key phrases, together with a slight nod, are simple, encouraging cues that prompt the speaker to continue talking.

Repetition of key words and restatement of key phrases is non-threatening. They provide a basis for agreement between the speaker and listener and stimulates further conversation. As the listener, take the opportunity to practice repetition of key words:

Speaker:	I had an interesting day!
Listener:	_____
Speaker:	That was an incredible meeting.
Listener:	_____

Now take the opportunity to practice restatement of key phrases:

Speaker:	I can't stand it when she turns her back on me.
Listener:	_____
Speaker:	I decided to change my mind.
Listener:	_____

When you listen your communication becomes consistent and direct.

Communication that is easily understood is more likely to be accepted. Although active listening seems obvious, *stating the obvious* is sometimes the most difficult thing to do. When you listen and respond in an objective, non-judgmental way, you help the speaker to accurately listen to his/her inner feelings. By effectively using non-judgmental statements, the listener checks out whether or not his/her perceptions are correct. Examples of non-judgmental statements to others are:

It seems to me that you're happy with your new relationship.

I believe that you're unsure about what your professor wants from you.

Based on my observation you're fond of Kirsten.

What I hear you saying is
_____

It is my perception that
_____

It is my impression that
_____

Non-judgmental statements let the speaker confirm or reject your perception. Carl Rogers (1961) wrote, "The major barrier to mutual interpersonal communication is our very natural tendency to judge, evaluate, to approve or disapprove, the statements of the other person or group." When you, as the listener, become less evaluative and more accepting, you help the speaker to become more self-expressive, self-aware, and open-minded.

Non-evaluative communication and active listening increase trust, understanding, self-worth, and self-confidence. When you actively listen, you focus and concentrate on what the other person is really saying. You can check out how accurate you are by asking, "Do I hear you correctly? Is that what you mean?" If you're perceived as not being accurate, try again. If you get the message that you are accurate, continue. Active listening motivates and encourages others. It bridges the gap in human communication.

Make Good Eye Contact to Show Interest

In the previous section on active listening, I discussed how you listen to the person and reflect back a word or phrase that emphasizes a feeling. People also judge how you listen, however, by looking at your eyes. Why is this important? Making good eye contact (1) focuses your, and the other person's, attention, (2) reduces distractions, and (3) encourages the speaker.

Encouraging listeners make more eye contact to facilitate conversations. They continually show involvement in the communication process. Forty-five percent of the time you pay attention and focus in on the verbal content (i.e., sounds, vocal qualities and tones, words) to the messages of others. When others want to communicate and make contact with you, take an interest in hearing what they have to say. If the time and place are not right for you to listen, be honest and let them know that another time would be more convenient. Erratic eye movements, or looking abruptly away from others, speak loud and clear and echo your intentions and feelings. Timing, concentration, and duration of eye contact gives both parties insight into their feelings. There is no replacement for honesty. Others will appreciate your openness, and respect your sincerity.

Fifty-five percent of the time you pay attention and focus in on the nonverbal content (i.e., body gestures, facial expressions, eye movements, posture, distance/proximity, clothing, dress and appearance) to the messages of others. Your eyes give you the greatest, yet most subtle of all conversational cues. Your pupils transmit information about your true feelings and emotions. Expression of positive emotions such as physical attraction, liking, and trust is conveyed by an expansion of the pupil. A restriction of the pupil may convey indifference, fear or neutrality.

Attraction between you and another person is communicated by allowing your gaze to remain fixed on each other for a second or two longer than usual. Know when to glance away. Inappropriate eye contact, or staring, can hinder good communication. If a person is in a superior/subordinate relationship, staring can provoke anger between two people. A stare can mean many things: "I'm pleasing to you," "Maybe I'm curious," or "Is there something wrong with me?" Show interest through eye contact that's enthusiastic. When you allow others to express themselves, without fear of ridicule, you facilitate their growth as unique persons. Honest communication provides individuals with a sense of purpose and significance.

Frederick S. Perls (1969), the noted gestalt psychologist, accurately observed, "Without communication, there cannot be contact, only isolation and boredom." To understand communication completely, you must be able to send and receive messages. How? Be consistent and unambiguous in what you say and do. For example, statements such as "I understand what you're saying and what you mean" clearly send the message that you are listening. Listening to what others are saying, and observing their behavior, will help you interact in a more congruent and effective way.

Take this opportunity to express yourself through your eyes. Look in a mirror. How many ways can you express Love, Concern, Hurt, Anger, Joy, Enthusiasm and any other emotion you care to convey to others? Write your experiences or feelings down on paper. Look in the mirror and imagine how someone else might feel if you looked at him/her with that expression on your face. Or try this out with friends and ask them to record their feelings as you model each expression.

When you communicate, make sure your message is accurately received and understood. When expressing a positive emotion, your eye-contact, or gaze, must reflect sincerity and trust. How do you reflect sincerity when you make eye contact with others? Take a moment to write it down.

_____

_____

_____

The clearer you are about what you feel, the clearer will be your nonverbal and verbal messages to others. You communicate successfully when you actively listen, make good eye contact, and respond with empathy.

Observe Body Language and
Take in the Whole Picture When Listening

When making sincere eye contact with others, do you reflect sincerity in your body gestures? Or do your eyes contradict your body language? You communicate messages to others through your body language, your outer image. This happens whether you're aware of it or not. In fact, the way others 'see you' influences their opinion of you. The way you present yourself influences others' perceptions of "who you are." Initially, your body language, or outer image appearance, is the only information others have in order to understand you. Project yourself as confidently and assuredly as possible.

Observing and paying attention to nonverbal communication, or body language, is perhaps one of the most important skills you can learn. When someone is expressing anger and slams the door at the same time, you can say that his actions are congruent (harmonious). However when someone states that they love you but turns his head everytime you speak with him, or sits in a closed, crossed-arm position, you might say that his behavior is incongruent (nonharmonious).

Consider the following example. Amy and John are introduced to each other by a mutual friend who thinks that they may like to get to know each other. John obviously likes Amy and asks her out to dinner for the following weekend. Amy doesn't want to displease their friend, or disappoint John, so she says, "I'd love to have dinner with you this weekend." Amy is really thinking that she'd rather not. When they're at dinner, John is hurt and frustrated when Amy acts distant and uninterested. He asks, "Is there something wrong?" Amy looks away and in a despondent voice says, "No, I'm just not hungry."

Obviously, Amy's tone of voice and behavior contradict what she really feels. She's acting in an incongruent fashion. If Amy had said, "I accepted your invitation because I didn't want to disappoint you or my friend," or "I was surprised at myself when I said Yes but meant No," then Amy would be acting congruently. Congruent communication leads to understanding and trust. Incongruent communication can breed mistrust and hostility, and lead to ambiguity and tension.

It's important to listen to the sound of the person's voice, not just his or her words. Pay attention to what the other person's body movement and posture tell you. When you are inconsistent in your communication others may resist and reject you more often. When you are consistent in your communication others value, believe and accept what you have to say. Communicating in a consistent, direct and honest way creates encouraging relationships in which the person feels his/her ideas and words have been heard and understood.

What benefits are people trying to achieve by certain behaviors? How do they go about behaving to make their point?

What do the following behaviors say to you? Write your responses in the area provided. Use action words.

Behavior	Interpretation
Hesitant movements?	_____
Backing away?	_____
Constant eye contact?	_____
Easy fluid walk?	_____
Arms folded?	_____

Yawning? _____

Raised Eyebrow? _____

The above behaviors may have different meanings in different situations. A raised eyebrow can suggest frustration or criticism with a situation. However, the same gesture in a business meeting with a competitor can mean, "What is he really saying? I had better analyze the situation before making a commitment."

It's a well known fact that gestures and facial expressions communicate varying degrees of like/dislike, approval/ disapproval, and agreement/disagreement. When observing behavior, don't conclude that your first impression is necessarily the right one. Judging and evaluating incorrectly distance you and others from developing trust. Check out your perceptions by first commenting on what you see a person doing (the behavior). Next, comment on what you sense a person is feeling. This is explained in detail in the next section.

Seeing versus Imagining

What you "see" is something that is observed in another's behavior. What you "imagine" is something that you suppose, guess or think. It's something that you assume that may or may not be true. First, state to the person what you see. For example, "I see you yawning." Second, state what you imagine. "I imagine you're bored." Let them tell you whether you're correct or not. You may be surprised to find out that sometimes what you've imagined is not necessarily the case.

Focus your communication on what you observe in the other person's behavior. The person's response to the previous example may be, "No, I'm not bored, I just need more oxygen, it's stuffy in this room." Acting on what you 'imagine' the person to be feeling or thinking may not be 100 percent accurate. This can result in confusion and produce miscommunications in your relationships.

Comment on what you imagine the following behaviors mean. Remember, your answer is an interpretation of the physical behavior.

I see your legs are crossed.   *I imagine* _____ .

I see your eyes fluttering.   *I imagine* _____ .

I see you scratching your arm.   *I imagine* _____ .

Is it possible to *see* a person being nervous? No. You can't see nervousness. However, you can imagine that the person is nervous. What you see is a behavior or an action that resembles "nervousness." Your interpretation of a behavior, or action, can be translated in many ways. The person may in fact be excited. How will the other person respond to you when you respond to the person "as if" he/she is nervous? He/she may respond in a confused way. However, stating what "you imagine," before jumping to conclusions, will change what you say, think and do before moving forward in communicating with others. Asking questions pertaining to another's behavior, or intent, will help you become more effective in your communication.

You can clear up a great deal of the confusion that goes on in interpersonal communication by using this simple technique. Remember, you are not a mind reader. Let the other person give you feedback on the accuracy or inaccuracy of your impressions. That's his/her responsibility. There's no guarantee that others will be straightforward. However, being clear and direct will encourage others to speak freely and sincerely.

Understanding the true meaning in the other person's behavior helps you to respond in a more focused and exact way. Choose to open the lines in communication by deciding to check out the accuracy of your perceptions. You'll be satisfied with the results. Don't assume anything.

Vocal Tone and Posture

What role does vocal tone and posture play in understanding yourself and others? When you listen to and focus in on the tone in the other person's voice, you'll be able to perceive the speaker's verbal and nonverbal message. Volume, tempo, and fluctuations in a person's voice can convey messages varying in degree and kind. The intensity in volume and tempo can clarify, and help you understand, sensitive issues and concerns others may be experiencing.

When you actively listen, the sounds in a person's voice will tell you a story or paint you a picture. Tuning-in to, and understanding, the subtle changes in a person's vocal tone and posture can give you clues about their private world of feelings. Tone, posture, and gesture play an important part in the development of communication and self-esteem.

Although the sounds produced by the jazz saxophone and rock

guitar are definitely different, both instruments can replicate sounds that resemble sorrow and grief or ecstacy and joy. Changes in the person's voice and posture are similar to the changes in the sounds made by these instruments. Pay attention to the sound and movement. Allow your senses the freedom to accept the impressions you receive while observing the whole picture—the whole person. The image of what the person communicates, and how it is communicated, will resonate loudly and clearly.

The more congruent (matched) the person's voice is to his posture, the more accurate and clear will be the person's message and motivation. Pleasant, melodic vocal tones and open postures usually indicate acceptance and trustworthiness. For example, the message "I love you," given with positive tone and posture, reflects an openness from the sender. This is congruent (matched) behavior.

There are times, however, when you will receive what is known as a mixed message—sounds that come from the person's voice that differ from his physical movement and posture, or from the words themselves. The more incongruent (mismatched) the person's voice is with his posture or words, the more inaccurate and unclear the person's message. A person who has a sweet sounding voice and states, "You really make me ill," is an example of a mixed message, a statement that's contradicted by the tone. Another example is a person using a harsh vocal tone, and closed posture, shouting, "You know I love you. Why are you questioning me?"

Before and while attending graduate school, I worked as a cosmetologist in several beauty salons to finance my graduate studies. I was fascinated with the different types of communication between clients and stylists. One time I had just finished an elegant hairstyle that the client had requested from a fashion magazine. For no apparent reason, the client picked up the brush and started recombing it. I asked, "Are you unhappy with the style or the way I cut your hair?" She answered me with the sweetest voice, a pleasant smile, and her head looking at the floor, "Oh, nothing is wrong; I'm very pleased with my hair." She continued brushing her hair and smiling.

A mixed message? Yes. The message would have been more straightforward and congruent if she had stated that she was experimenting with new styles for herself but that she was not going to wear it out of the salon. This was actually the case. Or, it would have been more congruent if she had said, "I really like the cut and style but my husband is disapproving of changes in my hairstyle.'' This statement clarifies the client's intent and motivation, and the discomfort she may be experiencing in her relationship. It was my responsibility to *listen* and *empathize,* not give advice.

Here is another example. A young man rushes over to his girlfriend and hugs her. Instead of the feeling being reciprocated, his girlfriend stiffens and turns her head. He backs away. She then states in a concerned voice, ''What's wrong honey? Don't you love me?'' The boyfriend moves toward her again, and hugs her only to receive the same gesture—pulling away and stiffening of the arm where he's holding her. He then responds by moving away from her. She says again, ''Honey, don't you love me? Why are you stepping back from me?''

The confused boyfriend is receiving a mixed message. The tone in his girfriend's voice sounds concerned, but she behaves in a cold, detached way. Here are two ways the scenario can go: One, he can let the situation stay the way it is without responding; or, two, he can comment on her behavior and voice stating, ''You sound caring, but when I touch you, you pull away and that gives me the message that you don't want to be touched. I feel that you would rather not be with me, and I'm hurt and confused.''

The second way is the preferable one. The boyfriend has made a clear statement about his girlfriend's behavior. He is able to comment on the mismatch in behavior and tone of voice. When you can communicate about the incongruity (disharmony) between a person's tone of voice and their behavior, you clarify your own feelings and reduce confusion. This can eliminate stress and anxiety depending on the actions taken to correct the conflict. Recognizing nonverbal behaviors and vocal tones that are mismatched, and being able to communicate about them, is learning how to state the obvious when clarifying mixed messages.

The following statements are congruent (matched) and incongruent (mismatched) messages. How would you describe your body posture and vocal tone in the space provided?

Statement	Vocal Tone	Posture
Example: I love you. (congruent)	Soft, melodic, moderate tone.	Open arms, good eye contact.
I love you. (incongruent)	Soft, melodic, moderate tone.	Closed arms and hands, eyes squinting.
I'd love to have dinner with you. (congruent)	_____	_____
I'd love to have dinner with you. (incongruent)	_____	_____
I'm really excited about working with you on this project. (congruent)	_____	_____
I'm really excited about working with you on this project. (incongruent)	_____	_____

When you *state the obvious,* and become more congruent in your communications, you take a giant step toward *communicating with confidence.* Communication that's confident and clear helps you get your point across. It also helps others understand their own communication and behavior. Feelings of self-worth, self-esteem and self-confidence are increased when you are recognized for your clear, consistent communication.

Take charge of your communication. Experience yourself, and others, from a new perspective. Your attitude and communication are two of the most important assets that you possess. They influence how you respond to others and how others will respond to you. The quality of your life is greatly influenced by the quality of your communication, first to yourself and then to others.

Proactive Versus Reactive Responding

We can become more capable and successful in relating to others when we choose to develop proactive rather than reactive communication. Proactive responding facilitates communication while reactive responding inhibits communication.

Proactive responding is the ability to *listen* to the other person's feelings and *empathize* without taking responsibility for those feelings. Taking responsibility for someone else's feelings creates undue emotional and mental stress. Ultimately, you're more apt to respond in a reactive way, projecting your pent-up frustrations or hostile feelings on others. Reactive communication blocks freedom of expression of others. When freedom of expression is blocked, it's like being submerged in water and drowning. When you fight to reach the surface and take a deep breath, first you're relieved and then your body relaxes.

Freedom of expression is just as important as breathing in life-giving oxygen. The ability to freely express yourself, in a proactive way, is essential when establishing two-way communication and building mutual trust. Blocking, or stifling, personal expression by discouraging yourself, or the communication of others, creates defensiveness and hostility within the person.

Reactive responding is unrewarding and discourages further communication. When you cut off communication, it's like slamming a door in the other person's face. If you've ever had a door slammed in your face, literally or figuratively, then you know it is not a pleasant feeling. Reactive responding creates conflict and resentment often leading to distrust and hostility.

Defensive communication may be a reaction to being held back or repressed in some way. Defensive, reactive communication erects barriers and creates resistances that close off and terminate communication. Trying to speak with someone about commitment in a relationship when the person is unsure about his/her feelings is difficult. When the person is noncommittal, your choice is to either act, or react. When someone finds it difficult to speak with you, you might react by blaming him; "It's his fault," "He's acting in a childish way," and so on.

Reactive communication constructs walls and roadblocks preventing us from understanding ourselves and others. A reactive response discourages and blocks further communication.

Non-defensive communication allows you to express yourself in an open, honest and straightforward way. When you communicate to others in a *proactive way,* you become more *responsive* to the needs of others. Proactive communication helps to break down the walls and barriers that prevent us from communicating more effectively. When you're proactive, you communicate with empathy. *Communicating with empathy encourages mutual feedback and shows genuine enthusiasm. Listening to feelings and responding congruently* to others are two of the best ways to develop healthier communications and behaviors within relationships.

A proactive response tells the other person you're still interested in keeping the lines of communication open. When you respond in a proactive way you would say, "Do you need some time to think about the level of commitment in our relationship? . . . sometimes new ideas take time to digest." Or, "You feel uncomfortable discussing commitment . . . let's talk about your feelings . . . give me an answer when you've had time to think about our relationship." A proactive response encourages further communication and rewards both you and the other person in the dialogue. Proactive communication builds trust and respect.

Positive communication encourages positive behavior. A compliment can positively motivate you to risk responding in an interested, rather than a disinterested way. When you're interested, you're motivated to make positive contact with others. Responding to others in a proactive way allows them the freedom to respond, or not respond, to you. You, as a proactive responder, can give this message: "I'm listening to you, and want to respond to you, and have you respond to me. However, if you're not ready I'm willing to postpone my need to communicate and continue our conversation at another time."

As a proactive responder, your attitude is one of growth, not stagnation. You make positive contact with others and believe that your effort to listen and communicate is respected.

Fine-tune your communication skills. Respond to the following statements in a proactive and a reactive way. Pay attention to your feelings.

Statement	**Response**
Example:	
1. I find it difficult to communicate with you.	*Reactive:* So, don't bother. *Proactive:* It may be difficult but I would like to listen to you.
2. We've been dating for two years and haven't had a discussion concerning long-range plans.	*Reactive:* _____ _____ *Proactive:* _____ _____

3. I'll try to express myself
   more often. I seem to be
   having a real difficult time
   conveying my emotions to
   you.

Reactive: _____

_____

Proactive: _____

_____

Remember, focus on *what* is being said rather than *why* it is being said. Aspects of communication that focus on the *what* (what is being said), *how* (how it is being said; nonverbals, vocal tone, etc.), *when* (timing), and *where* (location or context), help you gain true insight and understand the person's motivations. Focus on *what* you want to say and *how* you want to say it. When you give yourself time to respond in a proactive way, you get your point across in a clear, concise, and productive manner.

By changing what you say and how you say it, you can change and influence the communication and behavior of others. You can also improve proactive communication by changing your passive, negative communication into more responsible, active, and positive communication. Note the following examples.

Passive, Negative Communication	**Active, Positive Communication**
She always feels so hurt and devastated every time I comment her new career is below her.	She will feel, and respond, more positively toward me when I point out the advantages and disadvantages of her new career move.
I'm overweight.	I'm in the process of eating healthier and exercising.
He hurt my feelings.	I'm in control of my feelings and choose whether or not he will affect me.
If I keep hoping and waiting, something positive is bound to happen.	When I take action, I become more involved, and seek positive outcomes.

(Passive/Negative)

If I take your advice and I fail, it won't be my fault; it will be yours.

If I avoid my problems, they'll go away.

(Active/Positive)

I am responsible for the outcome of making my own decisions, and managing my emotions.

I can and will take steps to find solutions to my problems!

Take the opportunity to change some of your passive statements into more active communications.

Passive	*Active*
_____	_____
_____	_____
_____	_____
_____	_____
_____	_____
_____	_____

Master your communication and behavior. First decide what's important to you to make optimal changes that will lead you to take positive, congruent action. When your perceptions of who you are and what you do change, you change!

Consistently changing your negative communication by replacing it with positive, uplifting communication, will create feelings of greater self-confidence, self-worth, and motivation.

Become an encouraging and motivating force for yourself and others. Your positive, proactive communication is the key that turns on the ignition for your drive to success. Making positive changes in your life, and in your communication, are key for becoming more self-directing, understanding, accepting, and responsive.

Put yourself on a direct route to the destination of your choice. Move forward on the expressway of life!

Implicit Messages

To quote Mark Twain, "The difference between the right word and the almost right word is the difference between lightning and the lightning bug." There is a great difference indeed between what a person *intends* to say and what a person may actually say. An implicit message is one in which communication is not plainly expressed. It is implied. Implicit messages can entangle the real or intended message.

Implicit, or unspoken, messages can cause others to feel frustrated, confused or angry. When you receive implicit or hidden messages in the communications of others, it can confuse future communication. That's why it's important to say what you mean and mean what you say. For example, the implicit message in the sentence, "My stomach is rumbling," could translate into the explicit message, "I'm hungry. When are we going to eat?"

If you adopt this unproductive and discouraging way of communicating by using implicit messages, your relationships may not be as fulfilling as you would like them to be. For example, after a disagreement during a discussion you are sitting next to the person with whom you are in a relationship. She states, "I'm cold." She then moves away from you and wraps herself in a comforter. There can be a certain meaning or expectation *implied* in her message, and/or she may be disguising her own feelings of insecurity. Your perception is that she is withdrawing from you and insulating herself with the comforter. Your explicit message would be, "I'm feeling distant, anxious, and insecure after our disagreement." This explicit message clearly states the person's feelings and allows an opportunity for further discussion. Concealed, or implicit, messages disguise the person's real emotions which may cause future complications.

Take personal responsibility for clarifying implicit messages to prevent the development of walls and barriers to communication. Don't let hidden messages become the rule rather than the exception. Make the implicit (unspoken), explicit (spoken). Clearly state what you mean without reservation or disguise. Leave nothing implied. You can check out what the person feels by directly asking them, "Are you feeling distant and uncomfortable after our discussion? I'd like to clear up what's going on between us." Checking out the intended meaning in the message (e.g. "I'm cold") will facilitate productive communication and congruent behavior, resulting in healthier relationships.

Start now! Don't allow your future decisions and feelings to be controlled by unproductive past experiences. Now is the time to courageously move forward and change your unproductive, past communications.

What are some of the advantages of deleting implicit messages and communicating with others in a more active, straightforward and responsible way? What do you gain? Write your comments in below.

Develop greater self-respect by becoming more capable and responsible for communicating with clarity, consistency, and decisiveness. Get in touch with your optimism and courage to overcome your incongruent, self-defeating communication and behavior. Use your empathy and communication skills to develop the new, success-focused you! Your potential is unlimited!

Empathizing allows you to listen to others and be there for them, emotionally. When you empathize, you allow others safety in an otherwise risky situation. Understanding another person and accepting them, unconditionally, is important when communicating empathy.

Imagine being in a boat with a friend who is sailing for the first time. You are navigating in choppy waters with strong, gusty winds. You must reach the dock but to get there you have to go through a channel. Your friend turns and says to you, "I'm scared." You reply, "I understand. You are uneasy because this is new to you. I've been through this before and we are going to be fine." This empathic statement provides understanding, acceptance, and encouragement.

Lewis E. Losoncy (1977) wrote: "You as an encourager should be aware of how vital are your reactions to the discouraged person's ideas" (p. 94). Losoncy goes on to say, "After all, this person 'took a risk' and told you. This is healthy and a real compliment to you. An enthusiastic response will give the person the courage to take a risk again. Your reaction to what he/she says may determine whether or not this person pursues goals (growth) or gives them up (stagnation). Keep in mind that a comment uttered in a monotone or with a disinterested facial expression can really discourage someone who is already in doubt about his/her abilities and worth'' (p. 94).

When you empathize, you are not responding from a selfish, self-centered approach. You listen to, and understand, how the other person really feels. It's as if you can "stand in their shoes" and sense what the person is experiencing. As your ability to develop empathy improves, you begin to understand what it's like to see through the eyes, and feel through the heart, of others. Communicating something of that understanding to the person helps him accept and manage his personal feelings.

When you convey warmth and empathy toward others, you must first ask yourself, "What is the person trying to say to me?" Prefix your comments with such phrases as: "What I hear you saying is . . . You feel . . . If I understand you correctly." Statements such as these lets the other person know you want to listen.

Statement:	I had a major disagreement with my parents about dating.
Paraphrase:	What I hear you saying is that your parents' opinion about dating differs from yours.

Second, await verification.

Statement:	Yes, they didn't hear a word I said.
Paraphrase:	You felt they were not listening to you.
Statement:	And, that's not the only time this happened.

Third, capture the essence of what you hear and paraphrase this so the other person can verify or disclaim it in his/her intended message.

Paraphrase:	You feel hurt and upset about the lack of communication between you and your parents.
Statement:	Yes, I just want them to listen to me, and hear my side of the story, and accept that I have feelings also.
Paraphrase:	What I hear you saying is listening and having your feelings acknowledged by your parents is important to you.
Statement:	Yes, I just want them to hear what I have to say, before agreeing or disagreeing with me.

If the person indicates that your paraphrase was not the intended message, continue to listen and paraphrase until he/she verifies that you have heard correctly.

Empathic listening helps you build feelings of self-acceptance and self-worth. It manifests caring or concern instead of antagonism and rejection. When you paraphrase, there is no need to analyze what the person is saying. Simply re-phrase in your own words, or mirror, what you hear or think the person is saying. Here's another example:

Statement:	People always laugh at my ideas.
Paraphrase:	What you're saying is that you feel you are not taken seriously.

Now, take a few minutes and consider how you would paraphrase the following statements:

Statement: I give up, math is not my subject.

Paraphrase: _____

_____

Statement: They criticize me at parties because I don't drink alcohol.

Paraphrase: _____

_____

Statement: My friends told me I'd never make it in professional sports. They're probably right.

Paraphrase: _____

_____

Statement: I feel great! Life is an exciting challenge!

Paraphrase: _____

_____

Empathizing means you must first see others through your own eyes and your own heart. Imagine yourself in the other person's situation. Only then will you understand what it must be like for them to experience feelings and life's challenges. Empathy conveys the feeling that *you are worth listening to, and that I respect you enough to give you my undivided attention.* When others feel they have a safe place to communicate, their self-esteem grows. Your own enthusiasm and self-esteem will grow because your perception of your abilities changes. You can now communicate more effectively.

Listening to others helps you tune-in to your own feelings. Conveying to others what you think they're saying helps them tune-in to their thoughts and feelings. It is your decision to choose whether or not you want to empathize with others. However, when we cultivate the habit of empathizing deliberately, our understanding and compassion will steadily grow stronger. Becoming empathic helps you develop your abilities as a caring, compassionate and reassuring person.

Use the Power of Language

• Use of 'I' vs. 'You'

Using "You" when you mean "I," creates barriers in the communication process. Saying "You" but meaning "I" is one way of not taking responsibility for your experiences and feelings. How many times have you been in a conversation with someone when he is talking about himself but he says; "You know how you feel when you're late?" . . . "You know how you get nervous when you speak in front of others?" . . . "You know how you feel when you try to learn math and you fail?" . . . "You know how you feel when you get stressed?"

You're probably thinking, "Why does he keep saying I'm doing such and such when he's really talking about himself?" Most of the time, this person is not even aware of what he is doing. I call this the *"fogging effect."*

Using the "generic You" is the language of powerlessness. It's a way of avoiding your feelings and declining responsibility for who you are. This "generic You" also assumes that the other person feels the way you do when, in reality, you probably have a totally different perspective about a situation—and different feelings. In fact, if you were to check on the feelings and perceptions of the other person, you'd find that most of the time his perspective differs from yours. When you take for granted that others feel as you do, and project only your feelings into the communication, you're likely to deemphasize their feelings while emphasizing your own. Miscommunication can develop because others may feel that their feelings are not respected, or you've taken license to "feel or think for them" without really having been given permission.

The "fogging effect," or using "You" when meaning "I," suggests a person may feel threatened or uneasy about making contact with others. You may first want to use your empathy skills to understand what the person is really saying. Next, your responsibility is to communicate that *what* he/she is saying may be different from what you are thinking or feeling. You might simply say, "Are you telling me that I'm feeling this way, or are you talking about your own feelings or thoughts?" At first, others may be resistant to changing their "generic You" to making "I" statements. Don't push them to change. Your responsibility is to let them know that you may or may not feel the way they do. Paraphrasing and reflecting back to others what they're saying is an excellent way to clarify communications.

Saying "I" when meaning "I" is not selfish nor egotistical communication. There is more accuracy when one says "I" because the use of "I" specifically identifies the speaker and listener in the communication process. Clarify your communication and personalize your message. This will help you to hear more of what you are saying, and what you mean to say. It will also help others respond in a more direct, straightforward, and authentic way.

A powerful motivation is to be able to communicate with another person. The language of power is more assertive. The use of "I" helps you to reestablish your sense of power, control, and identity. Taking control of your communication helps you to control what you say and do. To a great degree, your feelings and responses are created and determined by the use of the first person, the "I" in communication. By actively using "I" instead of "You," you start to manage your feelings and make your own choices. Becoming more aware and in charge of your own feelings helps you to become responsible for yourself, your communication, and your decisions.

Take this opportunity to become more assertive with your feelings. Use the "I" in your communication. Write in your responses.

Statement	***Response***
Example:	
You know how you stress yourself.	I allow myself to feel stressed.
You know how you want to be treated.	————————————
After a while, you know how you just want to express yourself!	————————————
You know how you feel when you take a stand.	————————————

Employing ''You'' when you mean ''I'' sabotages your communication, self-esteem, and self-confidence. Enhance your self-esteem and achieve the confidence you deserve by taking responsibility for your feelings. Become more assertive by stating ''I'' more often. Increase your energy, determination, and self-esteem by speaking up for what you believe in and what you want.

Direct communication means becoming a more direct you. It's a risk you can take and a decision only you can make. Encourage yourself, and others, to risk saying ''I'' more often. Change your communication and become more responsible for what you feel, think and do. Taking this necessary action will change your behavior and your self-image.

You have the right to stand up for yourself. Make your communication more effective and forceful. Move yourself in the direction toward achieving your goals as a successful and dynamic communicator. When you take responsibility for your beliefs, emotions and actions, you position yourself for success. Learn the communication skills that will give you the competitive edge for a happy and prosperous life.

- ## Use your imagination as an energy source for success and fulfillment

"Everyone must have a place to go for sanctuary . . . to know where to go for rejuvenation and solitude."

PETER ELIAS

Visualization will help you to discover more energy and joy as you tune-in to your inner self. It will also help you gain the competitive edge in your personal and professional relationships. *Visualization, or 'mental imaging,'* is a powerful skill that can be practiced regularly to improve your communication.

It is a process of relaxation in which you can consciously evoke desired sensations and images. It is as if you are watching yourself and your surroundings on an inner screen. When you allow yourself to visualize, you are giving signals to your body to either increase or decrease sensation. You are in control of your sensations of feeling, hearing, smelling, seeing, color and temperature. Therefore, when you visualize, you control your feelings and thoughts. It is important to communicate positive signals, feelings, or ideas to maximize pleasant thoughts and situations, and eliminate unpleasant thoughts or situations.

To practice visualization, first choose a place that is relatively quiet, and where you can be alone for fifteen to thirty-minutes. Close your eyes and concentrate on your breathing. Breathe deeply and calm your body. For practice, imagine yourself sitting on the beach watching the sunset over the ocean . . . listen to the sound of the wind and waves . . . feel the sun as it touches your face . . . see the blue sky, touch the rocks and sand, and focus on anything else that is pleasing to you. Upon completion open your eyes, relax, and get ready for the next segment.

Next, close your eyes and try to create as real an image of the actual situation that you want to change. Focus on what is in the background and the foreground of your surroundings. Now choose a behavior (habit), or a skill, that is important to you. Make sure that it's one that you want to modify or change. It may be a new skill that you want to improve upon such as public speaking. When you have the particular situation in mind, visualize your movements and begin to slow yourself down (breathing deeply). See (in your mind) yourself speaking in front of a group. Listen to what you are saying. Observe your nonverbal gestures. Visualize this segment as if it were in slow motion. Pay attention to your own movements and sounds.

Next, begin to change and correct your verbal and nonverbal behaviors that may be frustrating your communication and performance. Replace your unproductive actions with ones that are more appropriate to improving your skills and increasing your performance. With your eyes still closed, allow yourself to review the situation again, only this time in the normal speed and in the new way. Remember, pay close attention to your verbal and nonverbal communication. You should be filling yourself with feelings of confidence. Imagine the audience applauding.

When you have finished open your eyes. It may be important for you to write down certain parts of your experience. This form of *guided imagery* can be implemented on a regular basis. Practicing fifteen minutes a day and increasing your time, incrementally, to thirty minutes is recommended.

When practicing *visualization,* there are two prerequisites that are essential to increase your performance and communications and, at the same time, reduce stress. One, *set realistic goals.* An example of a realistic goal can be to improve communication with your friend or with a colleague. Imagine yourself performing or communicating at a level of high proficiency which you know and occasionally do reach. And, two, *set specific goals.* For example, choose a skill that you want to improve so you can mentally rehearse the skill precisely. When you want to improve communication with your friend, practice the skills of active listening, empathizing, and using ''I'' statements.

Fine-tuning your ability to communicate with and understand others will help you recharge and make full use of your mental, physical and emotional energy. This will help you to become more self-aware and greatly increase your focus in personal and professional situations.

The only ones who ever really achieve their dreams
are those who have them.

Learn to recognize your patterns of behavior that keep you from changing. Use your communication skills and practice visualization to change negative thoughts and actions into positive ones. Communicate with yourself and others concerning the behaviors you want to change. This will help others to become more aware of your intentions to change.

Realize that you're in charge of constructing the life you desire. You are in the driver's seat of your own personal change. Using and understanding the dynamics of communication is like knowing when to change your spark plugs for better engine performance, or your tires for better traction. Deciding to tune yourself up by using your empathy and communication skills empower you to make consistent, positive changes in your relationships and in your life. These skills will help you change ineffective habits and patterns in order to achieve your goals and become the person you desire.

Believe in Yourself!

A positive mental attitude and a positive self-image are two of the most precious resources that you possess. Your attitude and self-image determine your willingness to grow, change, take on new challenges, feel alive, and become courageous. Focus on your strengths and assets, and build the self-esteem and self-confidence that you deserve.

Take the I Can I Will challenge. Learn the skills for growth outlined in this chapter to assist you in improving your communication with yourself, and others. Begin today! Take an active stand and live each day fully. Influence yourself and others to make decisions that will create collective, mutual success. Walt Disney believed, ''All our dreams will come true when we have the courage to pursue them.''

You can and will make your dreams come true. Make this your year for developing the ''I Can I Will'' attitude!

3.
Barriers to Success and Detours Along the Way

C hoice and Decision Making were walking through Pine Valley when Choice said, "What will happen when we come to the crossroads? It always seems to create so much conflict when trying to decide which way to go."

Decision Making replied, "Truly indeed, when you know you are at the crossroads that is the time that you make all your choices. When you are truly centered, you will always be on the crossroads of life."

Are you hitch-hiking through life and waiting for someone to stop and give you a ride? When you travel by hitch-hiking do you wait at the crossroads and let the direction you take be determined by the direction the traffic is moving, or do you break away from the mainstream? You would be imposing a detour on yourself by letting someone else take you in an undesired direction. When you finally do get a ride are you dropped off closer to or further away from your destination?

If you choose to retreat from your own responsibilities and let others make decisions for you, you may be avoiding the opportunity for making positive life changes. Giving up control by letting others take you for a ride may lead you further away from your destination.

Reaching your destination in a timely manner may require assuming responsibility for your life. Choose the road that will help you become self-responsible. Overcoming detours and barriers to success means choosing your direction with determination. Forge your own way!

The question you must ask yourself is not whether the road is right or wrong, but rather how significant are the decisions and choices you make when you're standing on the crossroads.

You have the power to make choices and decisions that determine the direction you take. It is your choice and responsibility to become self-determined. Creating productive beliefs and actions determine the way you respond to others. Letting others make decisions for your life is a relinquishment of ''will.'' It is an invitation to discouragement and frustration causing a loss of self-worth. Realize that you create your actions, beliefs, and behaviors to attain personal success.

For example, when you're scheduled for an important meeting and you know it takes one hour to get there, do you procrastinate until the last minute to get directions, gasoline, and confront the bumper-to-bumper traffic? What prevents you from planning your trip and making the necessary arrangements beforehand? You know what is required to get to the meeting on time and the direction you need to take. Developing self-direction is encouraging. It requires that you become a self-determined rather than an environmentally determined person, seeking your life goals in a more responsible way.

Decide your way and determine the course of your travel. Choose the road that brings you closer to your destination, not the one that leaves you further away. Taking responsibility for the events and changes in your life make you a more active, involved human being. Becoming determined to overcome your detours to success means making your own decisions and taking positive action to achieve future goals.

A detour can be a fun learning experience and enlighten you to make changes in your life that are meaningful. Imagine, you are on your way home from school to write a research paper. On your way home you take a detour into the library. You meet some friends who want to go for a ride. Here, the detour can afford you the opportunity to successfully compliment your primary goal, which is to complete the research paper, or it can lead you further away from the intended destination of completing the paper and arriving home.

Depending on others to find out how worthwhile you are, or when and how to live your life, is a detour to growth. What detours prevent you from taking risks, initiating action, and achieving personal success?

_____

_____

_____

Do you determine your outlook in life or let others determine it for you? At one time or another you may have allowed others to determine your feelings and situations for you. There are times when you may get off the road to success by allowing others to construct barriers that stifle and prevent you from growing and coping with life's challenges. Or, you may impose detours on yourself.

Self-Imposed Detours and Barriers to Success

Self-Imposed Detours are road blocks that you construct to prevent you from accomplishing your goals. They can lead you away from taking action in your life, blocking your initiative to become self-responsible and self-determining. But most importantly, self-imposed detours immobilize and discourage you. When you're discouraged, you focus on your negative points and weaknesses while ignoring your strengths and assets. This creates barriers to growth.

Barriers such as fear of success, self-judgement, and self-guilt can limit your risk-taking abilities. Instead of courageously moving forward to overcome difficult situations, barriers can instill fear and self-defeating thoughts and emotions. Detours such as procrastination, and letting others make decisions for you, are self-imposed detours that get you off track and stifle and block initiative.

Barriers to success and self-imposed detours may also reduce opportunities for creating challenge or experiencing joy in your life. Self-imposed detours interfere with personal challenge and spontaneity that allow you to experience situations as something new and exciting. When you recognize that certain barriers and detours are self-created, you can begin to take action and create effective strategies to overcome them.

• Fear of Success

Becoming successful by obtaining a goal can obviously be a positive experience. You can also block your own success with feelings of being overwhelmed once you get close to the goal. If you allow yourself to become dominated by these unproductive feelings, your state of mind affects your actions. Allowing your feelings to affect you in this counterproductive way stifles your ability to become successful. When success does occur, you're not able to accept the feelings of joy and power associated with your accomplishments. Denying feelings of accomplishment and success will result in producing highly ineffective and self-sabotaging behaviors. The behaviors are self-sabotaging because you're responding opposite to what is required to reach your goals.

Fear of success occurs because negative self-talk and negative messages from others still dominate your beliefs and attitude. What is your chance of success or advancement if you allow others to affect your thoughts and behavior? Realize that your effort in eliminating negative self-talk and negative beliefs from others is aimed at improving your self-confidence. Developing your inner resources, your self-esteem and self-respect, will motivate you to accept feelings of success on a continual basis.

Bravely overcoming discouraging feelings about yourself by eliminating self-defeating words from your vocabulary is one way to overcome fear of success. Another way is to disregard self-defeating statements from others. Success is achieved by continually expressing positive self-talk directed toward developing your enthusiasm, self-esteem, and vitality. "I can do it," "Great job," "Well done," and "Right on," are expressions of your vitality, influencing the course of your life. Your self-esteem and vitality will help you overcome any barrier and self-defeating attitude.

Changing your way of thinking about success activates your courage to solve problems and achieve goals. Instead of letting your problems get the better of you, take control and energize your courage by saying, "I am determined to reach my goals," and "My self-confidence and self-respect are so strong that *I will* move forward in life." These courageous affirmations will enable you to master and take control of your emotional, mental, and physical qualities to create passion in your life.

Your commitment to eliminate fear of success, and change your thoughts and actions, is a personal choice. Although internal, negative self-talk and discouraging words from others seem to surround you, focus your thoughts and actions in positive, productive ways.

One day, I was returning home from a basketball game. The coach had suggested that I spend more time practicing my jump shots and rebounding. It was raining and I was feeling a little down because our team lost. As I turned the corner at Boylston Street, I took a detour into the Boston Public Library in Copley Square.

Brousing through the rows of books, I came across Sammy Davis Jr.'s book *Yes I Can.* I remember taking a seat in the large reading room. As I read the book, I became more inspired. Sammy Davis Jr.'s encouraging words lifted my spirits and made me realize that I was not alone in feeling discouraged. We can find encouragement by realizing that the road to success for others has also been filled with barriers and detours. However, when you persist and move forward with determination, you can penetrate the wall of discouragement and move through it. Encouraging words from others assist and challenge us to face barriers, and overcome them.

When you experience rough times, discouraging words from others or negative self-talk, don't let yourself get down. If others try to instill fear in you by making you think you can't accomplish what you set out to do, face the challenge and keep moving forward. Believe in yourself and use encouraging self-talk to help you become enthusiastic about changing your behavior and attitude.

When you focus on developing your strengths and abilities, you begin to realize that you're responsible for changing your self-image and making your decisions. Affirm your positive belief, I Can I Will, and change your actions, language, feelings, and thoughts in productive ways. Using the *Communication Skills for Growth,* as explained in Chapter Two, will help you to develop the courage to overcome fear of success. Exerting your maximum effort and energy in situations requiring your focus and concentration will create the stamina for developing your attitude for lifelong success.

What positive actions will you take to change your behavior?

_____

_____

_____

Ultimately, the answers that you need are within you. When you reinforce your healthy behaviors and communication, the unhealthy ones have little opportunity to reemerge. Now move in the direction that you choose!

• Self-Judgement

When you dismiss the positive feelings associated with accomplishment, it's easy to slip back into negative self-talk and sabotage your success. In this discouraged state, you may find it difficult to focus on or allow yourself to enjoy feelings of success as feelings of self-judgement then emerge. Talking to yourself in a negative way reinforces habitual, unhealthy behavior. A statement such as, *"Why forge ahead if I never get anywhere?"* reflects a lack of self-confidence and low self-esteem. The self-judgement involved in focusing on past failures, rather than past successes, keeps you in the shadows of uncertainty where there's no opportunity for growth.

When your self-confidence and sense of security are deficient, you may impose a detour on yourself to avoid taking challenges or risks. When a highly successful event does happen, you may believe that it's sheer luck. Self-talk and beliefs such as *"My effort has no effect on the outcome,"* may stem from previously programmed messages that you received from discouraging others.

Feelings of insecurity and a lack of self-confidence can influence you to try to control external events, including others. When you're busy trying to control external events, you may not be in control of yourself. For example, trying to control the way someone feels toward you can be very frustrating. You can't control the feelings of others, but you can be *in control* of the way you respond and behave toward them. Attempting to control everything or everyone around you, rather than managing your own feelings and behaviors, undermines your self-growth and awareness. The point is not to focus on stopping others on their road to success, but to focus on your own personal growth and success. Work at understanding and appreciating your strengths (e.g. integrity, perseverance, sound judgement, forthrightness) that are always available within you. Focus on developing your strengths to become enthusiastic and energetic. When you empower your mind and body to develop your personal strengths and resources, you enliven and strengthen your commitment to become successful.

Why sabotage yourself, or anyone else? Criticizing yourself un-

justly undermines your growth and success. Blaming and judging yourself because you're not able to manage other people's thoughts and feelings is self-sabotaging. Undermining the success of others creates barriers to friendly relations, making it more difficult to appreciate situations that offer positive growth and opportunity. The feelings of success generated between two or more people far outweigh the feelings created by sabotage and self-judgement.

Stop undermining yourself or others. Concentrate on your own road to success. Devote your time and energy to developing healthy thoughts and emotions. Take responsibility for your actions and move confidently toward your new opportunities.

One way to stop sabotaging yourself and remove, or change, negative barriers and self-imposed detours is to focus on a positive experience in your life: a positive experience, or situation, that you can associate with a feeling of well-being or calm. An enthusiastic or peaceful feeling can create a positive change in your attitude and perception. Positive changes in your mental and emotional states create healthy, consistent changes in your actions. Positive, consistent changes in your verbal communication and nonverbal behavior create dynamic changes in your relations with others, eliminating sabotage and self-judgement.

When you change your physical, emotional, and mental condition, consistently becoming the person you desire each day, your perspective on living changes. Taking a detour, or sidetrack, can be very positive and inspirational.

During the late 1980s, an adolescent humpback whale took a detour off his route from Alaska to Hawaii through the San Francisco Bay, apparently due to his curiosity. Although making friends along the way Humphrey, the humpback whale, reversed his direction once he entered the narrow Sacramento River and continued towards his primary goal, the waters of Hawaii. However, he did return one more time the next year on his self-imposed detour. There's a lot to see along the way.

Imagine, you are sitting on a grassy knoll and watching the Humpback whales breech in the blue, turquoise waters off the shores of Maui, Hawaii, realizing that the 3,000 mile journey from Alaska was completed without eating. What determination! Watching their majestic form as they rise from the waters, together with a backdrop of orange and purple reflecting on the soft clouds, will reenergize you. As you tune in to the movement of the whales and the changes taking place in the sky and on the horizon, you become one with the scenery—with the dance.

What past positive, inspirational experiences can you think of when your fear or insecurity threatens your success? Remember a time when you needed courage and found it within yourself to successfully overcome fear or insecurity. Other past positive, inspirations such as reading an encouraging book and listening to an inspirational speaker may elicit the positive emotions to neutralize fear and insecurity. List your examples here.

_____

_____

_____

Identifying your positive experiences are valuable resources for continual personal growth and self-awareness. Now that you have identified this resource, how can you apply them to encourage positive communication and behavior with others to overcome your fear or insecurity? For example, complimenting yourself and others for contributing and improving your skills at a sport, consistently validating your personal strengths and those of others, increasing your positive self-talk to affirm your self-worth, and eliminating self-sabotaging behaviors and behaviors that undermine others, will eliminate fear and insecurity to help you communicate more effectively with others.

What steps will you take to turn your detours into an exciting learning experience?

_____

_____

_____

You can change your future by changing your direction. Energize all your assets and encourage yourself to create positive experiences in your life. When you actively choose the most responsible alternatives for your life, you are then in a better position to direct your actions. Challenge yourself to take responsibility for eliminating destructive feelings of self-judgement. Realize that self-judgement takes too much time and energy and is a product of your unrealized goal. You can take control of your actions, feelings, and thoughts and empower yourself to accomplish your goals. Move forward on your road to success!

• Self-Guilt

Imposing feelings of guilt upon yourself is a detour that you may confront along the road to success. One way to remove the detour of self-guilt is to confront the person or situation in a proactive way. In chapter two, *Skills for Growth*, I discussed how proactive responding will help you to positively assert yourself while empathizing with the other person. The difference between a proactive and a reactive response is the difference between an offensive posture and a defensive one.

A reactive response delivers the message that you are upset and unwilling to discuss your situation or compromise to facilitate a solution. Staying with a person who creates unhealthy, blaming, confusing and nonharmonious communication is a detour. There is no need to impose a detour of guilt upon yourself once you have decided to leave the relationship. It may be time to cut off relations with that person and change your situation. Once you've made the decision to move on with your life, take action to do it. There's no magic to making relationships work. It takes a commitment to work on communication. You either communicate with each other or you close the lines of communication.

To respond proactively, you can begin by letting the person know that you value and care for him/her, however uncomfortable his/her behavior or communication makes you. He/she has the choice to respond to you, or not. Open communication can only happen when you, and the other person, make it to happen. Remember, your responsibility is communicating to others in a proactive way. This will help you free yourself from pent-up emotions or painful feelings of self-guilt. There's no need to harbor discomfort or hide your feelings. Opening the lines of communication, or ending the relationship, are equally valid approaches. Either can yield positive, healthy results. You can let go of the person, or relationship, in a compassionate way, and remain friends. It's a decision you can make in concert with another.

When you're in the process of changing your relationships with others, be clear about your destination and your goals. Making a sound decision and taking positive action will create healthy changes in your life. This is the optimum way to increase personal growth and awareness, accomplish your goals, and successfully reach your destination.

Your positive movement forward is the first step toward eliminating self-guilt while rediscovering self-respect and self-determination. Focusing on positive and exciting experiences in your life will motivate you to remove the barrier of self-guilt. Removing the thoughts that constrict and restrict you from growing and changing will remove the blocks that prevent you from becoming successful. Developing a confident and benevolent attitude, and becoming more congruent in your behavior, is a positive move forward. Taking an I Can I Will approach will help you overcome any self-defeating attitude.

Eliminate self-guilt. Allow yourself the freedom to experience the beauty and power that exist within you.

> Two roads diverged in a wood,
> and I—
> I took the one less traveled by,
> And that has made all the difference.
> —ROBERT FROST

• Getting off Track

When you know where you're going why would you let others, without a sense of direction, make all the decisions? Letting others make random decisions for you can create conflict, and will eventually steer you off course. When outside advice or ideas contribute to your progress, graciously accept the new information. If the new information interferes with your progress, let it go. When you procrastinate without thinking you avoid taking action. However, waiting and temporarily suspending your action will help you carefully plan and choose your goals and destination, moving you forward with your progress and accomplishments. You have the power within yourself to make your own decisions and determine your own destination.

Don't give others the power to influence your future decisions. Expanding the vision of your future eliminates the "forecast of failure" that others attempt to predict for you. Believing in a "failure forecast" is self-sabotaging. Besides, it limits your creativity and freedom. Don't let the narrow experiences of your past or others determine your destination.

Relinquishing your power to others allows them to influence your future decisions. Taking responsibility for your decisions and actions help you to reach two objectives. One, it encourages and challenges you to consistently improve yourself; and two, it empowers you to move forward with the conviction that you control your own life. Success is seeking your life goals in a more responsible, active way.

Imagine that you're coaching a team and your strategy isn't working. Would you stay with your present strategy, or change it to maximize your performance and chances at winning? You have the power, and 'will', to change your decisions and strategies. When your goals or plans need changing so as to maximize your happiness and peak performance, change them. You're the only one in charge of your future and your destiny. When you change your limiting beliefs and decisions into ones that are full of power, will, and energy, you create lasting, positive changes in your life.

Think about it. The quality of your life is enhanced by the decisions you make. Your personal power grows when you take charge of your decisions and make healthier ones. You become impeccable when you are unwavering in your purpose and skillful in making decisions. This increases your self-esteem and utilizes "free will."

Carlos Castaneda (1974) states in *Tales of Power,* "A warrior cannot be helpless, or bewildered or frightened, not under any circumstances. For a warrior there is time only for his impeccability; everything else drains his power, impeccability replenishes it" (p. 194). When you know you're headed in the right direction and all signs say "GO," keep moving in that direction. Continual procrastination without thought drains your power.

Remember, do your best in whatever you're engaged in—fine-tuning your relationship and personal growth skills, achieving excellence at a sport, mastering your emotional, physical, and professional life, and liberating yourself from the shackles of unhealthy beliefs will renew your power.

Directing yourself on the road to success means focusing on your target and staying on track. As the renowned Dr. Jonas Salk put it, "Never make the mistake of limiting the vision of your future by something as narrow as the experiences of your past."

• Thought Stopping

You have the choice to control negativity and self-sabotaging behavior by creating positive beliefs and envisioning positive outcomes. Through a practice called "thought stopping," you can change direction when you find yourself slipping into a negative thought pattern. Say to yourself, with a loud and firm inner voice: *STOP!* Once you've done this, it's important to replace your previous thought with a more positive statement and image. Clearly acknowledge which statements cause you to feel pain or threat, and which statements allow you to feel success, joy and happiness.

When people unnecessarily stress themselves by thinking that they have no control over a controllable situation, they need to use their inner voice to shout out the word "STOP." Then, change track and think about how the situation can be redirected.

Now, take this opportunity to practice "thought stopping." What reoccuring thought causes you to feel negative, or some form of discomfort, pain, or threat? (Example: Taking risks makes me feel anxious.) Write your example in this space.

_____

_____

_____

Now, with a loud and firm inner voice, shout out "STOP!" Again, "STOP!" Replace your negative feeling or thought with a positive statement. (Example: When I take risks I experience excitement, learn more about myself, and feel encouraged to risk again.)

_____

_____

_____

When you attach specific positive words to positive feelings and experiences, you can recall positive feelings at will by using those words. Now apply the positive affirmation for yourself. Using your positive statement, attach it to feelings of success, joy, and happiness. For example, "When I challenge and encourage myself, I consistently move toward my goals with a success attitude, 'I Can I Will.' "

Recite the statement to yourself several times. Each time, experience the positive feelings the statement generates. When you anchor positive words or statements to positive feelings, you can recall the positive feeling anytime you desire and create more positive outcomes, consistently.

Challenge yourself! Stop your self-sabotaging thoughts and behaviors. Practicing *thought stopping* on a continual basis allows you to eliminate negative thoughts to become more aware of your feelings of accomplishment, self-acceptance, and of positive choice and change. Your new, bright thoughts and feelings of pleasure, joy and happiness drive you toward your destination of success. Positive feelings and beliefs increase your self-worth and self-esteem, empowering you to take action.

When you're in charge of your decisions, you choose the best route to reach your destination. Once you begin to change yourself, you need to move forward with your decisions and your desires. Don't hesitate. Visualize your future and start taking active control of your own destiny.

It's your choice and your responsibility to energize yourself by accelerating positive changes in your life. It takes just as much time and energy to dismiss and disregard your feelings as it does understanding and taking responsibility for them. You become what you believe you will become. Irrational beliefs can create irrational feelings and actions. Developing positive beliefs and affirmations motivate you to subscribe to a vision of health and success.

Becoming aware of your thoughts and feelings helps you to discard what is unnecessary or detrimental and overcome barriers and self-imposed detours that prevent success. Know that your beliefs influence your feelings, just as your feelings can and will influence your beliefs and your actions. Believe in the power of optimistic thought. When you stand up for yourself and your rights, you become determined to succeed.

Limiting, or sabotaging, yourself and your success by consciously taking dead ends is a waste of valuable time. When you know that destructive communication and behavior causes disharmony, what do you gain if you don't change?

When you're off track and need to restabilize yourself, look at your map and change your strategy to take the course that is most advantageous for you. Create a win for yourself by choosing constructive, congruent communication rather than destructive, incongruent communication and behavior. An overall plan or vision of where you are headed will save you a lot of time and energy. It will also create the drive and "*will*" to succeed.

Commit yourself to long-term change and success by making your own decisions. Making your own decisions empowers you to raise your personal standards, becoming impeccable. Believing in yourself means believing and trusting your intuition. The three Chinese characters Tsu Shin Gen translated means, "The entire body must see what cannot be seen with the eyes and hear what cannot be heard with the ears, that is true insight." True insight helps you to live each moment to the fullest. It is the seed that transforms your life while teaching you how to achieve optimal health.

Believe in all your senses. And when you're at the crossroads, the decisions you make are going to take you where you need to be. Don't be alarmed by the power and energy generated by your self-confidence. Your growing "inner" confidence and self-esteem multiplies as your senses become charged for success. Awaken yourself to yourself. Awaken all your strengths and unique characteristics. Awaken your courage and intelligence. Awaken your analytical abilities and the feelings within your heart. Awaken your benevolence. Awaken your inner sense of "will," right now! Take a moment and complete the following statements for yourself:

I empower myself to awaken my _____.

I empower myself to awaken my _____.

I empower myself to awaken my _____.

Awaken yourself! Activate your awareness and open the doors to wisdom.

Now is the time to empower yourself with positive beliefs and affirmations. Create an impeccable vision of your future. You Can and you Will!

4.
Overcoming Barriers to Change

"Nothing great was ever achieved without enthusiasm."
—RALPH WALDO EMERSON

Choice and Decision Making continued speaking while walking down a road surrounded by pine trees and high mountains. Choice said to Decision Making, "What about the shackles around our minds and hearts? Are they also around our souls? Once you have been conditioned, are those the shackles that you must carry with you for the rest of your life? How would you shed them?"

Decision Making replied, "The East Indians believe that the elephant and the mouse are the most powerful animals in the world. The mouse, because of its small size, can go anywhere unnoticed. The elephant, because of its immense size and strength, can topple trees and clear a path wherever it wishes to roam."

Decision Making continued, "Have you ever seen an elephant at the circus or the zoo? You might notice that attached on their rear, left leg is a steel chain anklet. Connected to the anklet is a short nylon cord with a small, wood peg at the end of the cord. The trainer can walk over to the elephant's left ear, and direct the elephant over to a spot, then step on the wood peg and kick some dirt over it. The elephant will stand there and move its two front legs and its rear right leg, but it will not move its rear left leg, even if there is hay that is just slightly out of reach. The elephant will stretch to get the hay with its trunk, but it will only stretch its two front legs and the rear right leg. It will not move the rear, left leg. Why? When the elephant was a baby, the trainer put its first steel, chain anklet on its rear, left leg. The anklet was connected to a steel cable, that was connected to a six foot steel pole, which the trainer drove into the ground at a 30 degree angle.''

''No matter how hard that elephant tugged and tried to get away, it could not. Finally, the elephant gave up because his spirit was broken. Now, when the trainer takes the elephant and moves it by the ear, and brings him to a place to peg him, the elephant will remain in the designated area. He will not try one more time to move his left rear leg even though he is only one trial away from success. All that elephant has to do is pick up his leg, one more time, to learn that he can free himself of his restriction. He is only one step away from success.''

Some of us may be like the elephant. We may have experienced barriers that have kept us from changing and becoming successful. A negative attitude is a barrier that can restrict you from making healthy contact with others. Healthy contact is essential in the communication process. A negative attitude is like having a shackle around your heart and mind. This shackle, or negative attitude, is a barrier that can restrict you from growing and changing.

Growth and change are healthy functions of every human being. When growth and change are blocked for some reason, your ability to remain flexible and adjust to various situations is decreased.

Changing negative attitudes and expectations into positive ones is the first step to remove barriers to change. To achieve and accomplish the seemingly impossible, what mental, emotional, and physical barriers do you need to acknowledge and remove? Whether these barriers have been inflicted upon you by others, or yourself, take a moment to think about the above question. What examples of your own can you include in the space provided below:

What do you need to accomplish?

_____

_____

_____

What barriers do you need to remove?

_____

_____

_____

These barriers and attitudes can keep you from experiencing the positive effects of change.

For example, if I were to show you a map of the world, chances are you could find a place on it to visit. Feel the excitement of going on a vacation and visiting places you've never seen before. The fun is in the journey. Now, if I were to ask you how far you could drive on the U.S. continent, given unlimited mileage, gasoline, and determination, you would probably say 'from ocean to ocean.'

However, if I were to ask you how much you could achieve in your life given the same amount of unlimited determination and drive, would you have the same amount of optimism? If I were to ask you where you want to be two, four, six, or twelve months from now, would you know? How is it that you can develop your excitement for going on a two-week vacation, but give little thought to your personal goals or destiny? In the following pages, you'll discover how you put these emotional and physical barriers in the way toward achieving your goals. You'll also learn ways to remove the barriers that prevent you from enjoying and living life to its fullest.

Overcoming Inner Barriers

Inner barriers (i.e., self-guilt, self-judgement) can prevent and interrupt your flow of ideas and feelings. When you become aware of the ways in which you interrupt yourself, you become aware of what you interrupt and how you do it.

What personal behaviors cause you the most pain?

_____

_____

_____

What negative conditions in your life are you sure you won't change?

_____

_____

_____

What are some of the patterns in your life that you can change, but are unwilling to do so?

_____

_____

_____

Your answers to these questions hold the key to how you create inner barriers and avoid responsibility for taking personal action. Losoncy (1980) states, ''The unproductive way of viewing why you are the way you are today is to put the responsibility for your feelings, thoughts, and actions outside of yourself or to put blame, but not responsibility, on yourself'' (p. 16).

Four major inner barriers that are destructive and inhibit communication are: _negative preconceptions, barriers of fear, a false self-image,_ and _negative self-talk._ Other barriers include toxic relationships and negative communication. To remove these barriers you have to understand what they are and how they work. As you discover your barriers and negative preconceptions, you can then take the necessary measures and actions to remove them.

Overcoming Negative Preconceptions

A negative preconception is an unproductive way of viewing yourself. Preconceptions are previously formed opinions, or ideas, you have about yourself. These preformed opinions, or biases, about who you are can influence your future feelings and actions. The most significant way to determine whether or not you will succeed is whether your preconceptions are positive or negative. Negative preconceptions prevent you from motivating yourself. They also prevent you from taking positive action to change your self-image.

With barriers or unpleasant situations in your way, it's extremely difficult to see clearly enough to remove the obstacles. When barriers block your growth process, your self-worth and self-confidence are weakened. The opportunity to relate to, work with, or be acknowledged by others is diminished. Negative preconceptions are counterproductive, self-punishing, and unhelpful.

Your self-worth and self-confidence are strengthened when you're able to relate to others and be acknowledged in ways that you value and that cause you the least amount of discomfort. Once you eliminate negative preconceptions, you become aware of and begin to experience the kinds of relationships and situations that help you build your sense of self-esteem and self-confidence.

When you begin to discover situations that raise your self-worth and self-confidence, take advantage of those situations. Instead of saying to yourself, "What does it really matter," believe that you have control of changing your life and say, "I'm going for it," "I feel so optimistic that every situation is an exciting challenge," "I'm unstoppable." Change your negative vocabulary and self-talk into positive vocabulary and self-talk on a continual basis. Identifying statements that create negative emotions (i.e., anxiety, fear, and insecurity) and statements that create positive emotions (i.e., excitement, joy, and challenge) affords you the opportunity to change your statements to create positive emotional and mental states. Ultimately, this will change how you act toward others.

Involve yourself in healthy, optimistic situations that generate positive feelings. Positive situations can generate a well of resources, and will instill within you a sense of purpose, self-confidence and self-empowerment. Take responsibility for getting involved with people who are open-minded and who inspire you to grow and change. You can transform your thoughts and emotions by keeping your enthusiasm high. Your courage to move forward in a goal-oriented way begins with the belief that I Can I Will.

Choice and Decision Making went traveling down Sunrise Highway when Choice said, "Ultimately, you're in charge of your life and can transform every aspect of your emotional, mental and physical destiny."

"That's true," Decision Making replied as he stared into the violet, iridescent sunset. He continued, "It's also true that the goal and purpose of teaching and learning are to raise your own consciousness as well as the consciousness of others."

The sun melted into the mountains as they sat in silence.

Overcoming Barriers of Fear

Napoleon Hill (1960) affirms in *Think and Grow Rich,* "Fear of poverty is a state of mind, nothing else! But it is sufficient to destroy one's chances of achievement in any undertaking" (p. 224). He adds, "This fear paralyzes the faculty of reason, destroys the faculty of imagination, kills off self-reliance, undermines enthusiasm, destroys initiative, leads to uncertainty of purpose, encourages procrastination, wipes out enthusiasm and makes self-control an impossibility. It takes the charm from one's personality, destroys the possibility of accurate thinking, diverts concentration of effort . . . turns the will-power into nothingness, and destroys ambition" (p. 224).

Fears are inner barriers, or roadblocks, that can be removed by changing negative thoughts into positive ones to create positive action. Fears are fueled by a poor or negative self-image. Fear of making decisions, helplessness, fear of rejection, fear of failure, fear of your own greatness, and fear of your own talents are all behaviors, or conditions, that prevent you from changing.

For example, when you fear failure, your motivation is to avoid failure rather than to achieve or seek success. You can fear your best as well as your worst. These barriers will also prevent you from exerting yourself, not because you can't perform, but because you fear you can't perform well.

Imagine telling a significant role model in your life something new and exciting. An idea or event that has stimulated you both mentally and physically. It can be anything from trying out for a dramatic play, joining a sports team, beginning a new career, starting a new marriage, losing weight, developing a new outlook, changing your image, or continuing your education. Instead of receiving an encouraging comment, what you hear instead is: "That's ridiculous," "You're always daydreaming," or "You'll never make anything out of yourself."

Negative statements such as the ones mentioned above can create fear of failure and fear of rejection within a person. This situation can leave an individual on the receiving end feeling helpless. Negative attitudes create barriers toward individual accomplishment. The implicit, or unspoken message, is: "Whatever gave you the idea that you are motivated enough?."

Do you remember a time when you or a friend finally made the team but the coach left you sitting on the bench? What kinds of feelings did you experience? Humiliation? Insecurity? What will it take for you to get off of the bench and become the athlete, the person, you truly want to become. What's preventing you from speaking up and letting the coach know that you're one terrific person, and given the chance you'll prove just how unstoppable you really can become. Harvey Mackay states, "How can you be any good unless you think you can accomplish what you're not supposed to be able to accomplish?"

Sitting on the bench, and not asserting yourself, is like being in a play without acting out the part. Do you go through life without getting involved one-hundred percent? Maybe it's because you believe you might fail, or even succeed, at what you set out to accomplish. Do you set yourself up for failure and sabotage your success by telling yourself that you can't perform well? Is it possible that you allow unproductive and negative vocabulary to dominate your thoughts? Negative self-talk demotivates you and is an inner barrier that must be eliminated.

Change your mental and emotional state. A positive attitude will eliminate inner barriers and drive you toward accomplishing your personal goals. Here are some statements that characterize "fear of failure" and "need for achievement." Let's see how you can change passive (fear of failure) statements into more active, positive communications (need for achievement) by using upbeat, positive vocabulary. Changing your words can change and reset your attitude!

Passive Statements *Fear of Failure*	*Active Statements* *Need for Achievement*
I can't do it.	I'll try harder, and next time I will accomplish what I set out to do.
I better not go ahead with my idea, although it seems like a viable one.	I'll speak up and take action to give my ideas a fighting chance. If my idea needs to be modified to better fit the situation, the change will be welcomed.
I'll wait and hope my purpose in life comes to me.	I'm excited! I'll make a plan and move in a positive direction.
What if I don't lose weight? Then nothing will change.	I'll change my attitude and redefine the way I look and feel (by exercising and dieting).
It can't get much worse, nothing I do has any effect.	I chose the best plan given the circumstances. I'll continually improve my skills for success and next time my actions will lead to great results.
What if I don't get better?	I can and will get better. I'm unstoppable!

Here are three ways to overcome self-sabotaging behaviors and fear of success. One, continually tell yourself that you welcome challenges. Stand ready and willing to challenge yourself to your maximum capacity. Move forward in your communication by deleting all negative self-talk. The statements *"I can't," "I won't," "What if,"* and *"If only"* are unproductive and immobilizing. Substitute the statement *"I Can I Will"* for *"I can't"* or *"I won't."* This is more responsible language, empowering you to develop a more courageous and constructive approach to life.

Two, believe that whatever you set out to accomplish, you will give it one-hundred percent. Stop providing excuses to blame yourself, becoming disempowered from achieving your goals and increasing your self-esteem. Believe that your "pride of accomplishment" motivates you to eliminate all the "shoulds," "oughts," and "musts," from your vocabulary. You can reward yourself for any size achievement. Develop the courage to be yourself. You're one gifted individual.

And three, be the best you can. Continually "see" yourself in an evolving way. Stretch every mental, emotional, and physical fiber within you. Believe and feel that you are one dynamite, ecstatic, and powerful person. Remember, your beliefs impact the way you feel and act.

Now it's your chance! Reset your attitude! Change your passive language (fear of failure) into more positive communication (need for achievement). Learn to develop a winning attitude for personal success.

When Thomas Edison was in the process of experimenting with electricity, a *New York Times* reporter asked, "How does it feel to have failed seven hundred times [attempting to invent the electric light]?"

Edison responded, "I have not failed seven-hundred times. I have not failed once. I have succeeded in proving that those seven-hundred ways will not work. When I have eliminated the ways that will not work, I will find the way that will work." (from Harvey Mackay, *Beware the Naked Man Who Offers You His Shirt*, p.373).

Success is taking a "failure attitude" and turning it inside out. The first step in changing an attitude of failure into one of success is to change negative words into positive ones. Second, focus on constant self-improvement. Being obsessed with a wasted past does nothing but waste the present. Regrets are an exercise in futility which can go on forever, until you decide to make a change. It's imperative that you move forward. When you're moving forward and in gear, your attitude toward achievement becomes ignited. As you become more skilled in the use of positive communications, you begin to speak in optimistic language. Your personal success and optimism is reflected in your positive attitude.

Taking positive action and discovering what motivates you requires investing time and energy. It also involves taking risks. Venturing forth and taking a risk will help you overcome your initial fear and energize you to take action. When risk-taking is viewed as a challenge and a way to improve the quality of your life, it stimulates your mind and draws upon your inner strengths to creatively use the imagination.

Motivation, like imagination, determines your momentum. Your motivation to achieve is like a sparkplug. It causes an explosion and ignites the fuel that moves your pistons. Your momentum drives your "internal engine." However, if you fill your mind with disbelief, fear, or doubt concerning your abilities, your internal engine will work overtime in making these negative thoughts or beliefs a reality. When you fill your mind with courageous, optimistic, and confident beliefs about your abilities, your internal engine pulls you forward. Your internal engine, or drive, influences your thoughts and actions, and determines your personal success. Charles Garfield (1984) states in *Peak Performance:*

> Each of us possess a highly sophisticated and effective communications network between mind and body, a mechanism in which every change in the physiological state is accompanied by an appropriate change in the mental/emotional state, conscious or unconscious; and, conversely, every change in the mental/emotional state, conscious or unconscious, is accompanied by an appropriate change in the physiological state.

Conscious or unconscious thoughts influence behavior and behavior influences thoughts. Positive thoughts, such as, "I know I can," "I am capable," and "I am enthusiastic" will affirm your self-confidence and change your state of motivation and emotion. Positive motivation and emotion develops momentum. Encourage positive emotions to dominate your mind and eliminate negative ones. This can be accomplished by focusing your "will," or inner drive, to energize inner change. Volition, or will, is at the core of your inner self. Garfield (1984) adds, "The stronger and more constant your belief in volition, the more positive and consistent your efforts to succeed will be" (p. 40). Your "will" is the spark that increases self-esteem and drives you to excel and improve your performance.

Focus your "will" and decide which actions will help you overcome barriers to success. Choose only those situations and conditions that maximize positive emotion and energy. Avoid situations that blame, punish or impose guilt upon you. Your ability and desire to develop peak performance depend on your "will" and your self-discipline. When you discipline yourself and set goals, remember to establish realistic time frames for reaching them and evaluate your progress along the way. Consistently measure your progress.

Take control, now, and jump-start your life! Spark your "internal engine" to achieve, learn and grow. Realize and achieve your dreams. Your prescription for success is focusing on becoming the person you truly desire.

Overcoming a False Self-Image

It takes just about as much energy to create a positive self-image as it does to create a negative one. Think about it. Then why and how do people create false self-images? Fritz Perls (1950) suggested that when people dedicate their lives to actualizing a concept of what they should be like, rather than to actualizing themselves, they create a false self-image. This false self-image drives them head-on into a no-win situation.

Have you experienced a time when you said to yourself, "I should be like my mother, or my manager, or some famous actress, etc." Comparing yourself to others, thinking you "should" become someone other than who you are, is a barrier to growth. It's impossible to become exactly like someone else. In fact, trying to vicariously experience what someone else thinks and does is frustrating and counterproductive.

The difference between actualizing yourself and actualizing a false self-image is very important. When you actualize a false self-image you only live for your imaginary self. Perls (1969) notes, "Where some people have a self, most people have a void, because they are so busy projecting themselves as this or that. This is again the curse of the ideal. The curse that you should not be what you are" (p. 20).

Attempting to become someone or something that you're not can be discouraging and unhealthy. How can you project yourself confidently when you're not sure if it's the "real you" your projecting or a false self-image? When you create a false, or pretend, self-image, you're not actualizing who you are, just who you've imagined yourself to be. If you positively reinforce a 'mask' of who you think you are, you're only putting energy into the mask, or persona (imaginary self), not your real and authentic self. This kind of behavior creates a self-image of inadequacy and failure. Ultimately, the person will retreat and withdraw from situations offering positive growth and change.

Retreat or withdrawal usually occur when you set expectations for yourself that are unrealistic. Setting your sights too high can set you up for failure. If this is the case, you may retreat and decide not to bother with your original objectives. Then again, how do you know what you can or cannot accomplish if you're not sure who you're setting expectations for—your authentic or false self-image?

Unrealistic expectations and negative beliefs about what you can or cannot accomplish are barriers. These barriers reinforce failure. When you get caught up in your own failure 'script', you become predetermined to fail in everything you attempt. Your failure script is made up of negative beliefs that devalue you as a unique human being. Statements such as:

"I'm convinced that nobody really cares about me."

"I'll reject you before you have a chance to reject me."

"I'm basically unlovable."

"The world is filled with people who are likely to be rejecting. I must keep to myself, so I won't be hurt."

"My past must continue to control me today."

Statements such as the ones above are examples of self-limiting, negative beliefs and unrealistic expectations. Self-limiting beliefs and expectations can potentially lead to disaster. How can you know whether or not you can do something unless you try. Beliefs such as *"knowing things will rarely work out well,"* and *"feeling guilty about letting everyone down"* (including myself) are self-created no-win situations. Allowing yourself to become discouraged only reinforces negative beliefs and expectations. When you give up your purpose (the determination to move ahead), you stifle and prevent yourself from growing and coping with life's challenges.

Working to achieve realistic expectations, rather than living in fantasyland with a false self-image that masks your true self, promotes positive, personal growth and success. It's healthier and more beneficial to focus on and develop your own inner strengths and resources. Inner strengths such as integrity, honesty, and compassion, are essential in the process of maturation. Maturation is the ability to grow, confront, and become responsible for issues or problems in life. Maturing is also knowing when to remove barriers of negative beliefs and expectations that prevent you from developing self-respect and standing on your own feet.

Realize that one of your main goals is becoming a mature, self-actualized person. In the self-actualizing relationship, you are authentic and true to yourself, willing to accept yourself and others, uncondi- tionally. You have no "hidden agendas" or ulterior motives that reflect a need to manipulate or sabotage yourself and others. You're able to stand on your own feet and depend on yourself for developing respon- sible behaviors. Developing responsible behaviors means becoming more precise about what you want. Select actions to reinforce contin- ual self-improvement and personal growth.

Reward yourself for being the kind of person that sees the glass half-full, not half-empty. Your beliefs and your outlook in life impacts your choice and decision making. Focus your commitment and decide to create consistent behaviors and beliefs. When you empower your- self, your evolving self-image will pulsate with authenticity, self- encouragement and self-understanding.

Integrating Your Self-Image

Understanding and integrating your self-image is a powerful way to overcome any barrier to growth or change. Your "will" to unify and integrate your self-image and personality depends on the process of individuation. Carl Gustav Jung spoke about *individuation* as a process in which the person moves away from environmental support to self- support. The person becomes self-sufficient, determining his/her own way, rather than depending solely on others for support.

Individuated people are self-actualized and live in the present, accepting life for what it is, right now. As an individuated person, you're also influenced by your courage and willingness to change—the cour- age to accept yourself for who you are, and the willingness to change and become authentic and self-responsible. When you respect and trust yourself, you become fully responsible for your decisions and your life.

The process of individuation also helps you listen to your innermost needs. It helps you to become totally self-accepting and recognize yourself as a person with conviction. This conviction, or strong belief you have about yourself, means that you count and exist as a unique part of the human race. Once you commit yourself to higher achieve- ment, you act and speak in a more congruent way, and you're encour- aged to take more risks. When you make a commitment to achieve more financially, emotionally, mentally and physically, or find per- sonal meaning in your life, you become more enthusiastic. Your ability to concentrate also increases.

When you establish new perceptions about who you are, and what you want to achieve, you become more sensitive to your environment and to others. Becoming aware of your authentic self-image facilitates a dynamic, creative process through which you affirm yourself and give new meaning to your relationships with others.

Becoming aware of your authentic self-image awakens you to a new attitude. Your new attitude and positive self-image promotes changes in your habitual, routine way of doing things. Creating empowering beliefs and behaviors redefines your self-image, encouraging you to take positive action. Become aware of your self-determination and self-confidence that are always available within you. These qualities increase your ability to communicate more effectively and build relationships based on a concern for the growth, protection, and welfare of others. As you become more self-determined, you become more motivated to contribute to the welfare of others. You recognize ability and like to be recognized for your ability. Developing self-reliance and self-confidence, while actively and assertively helping others, is the mark of a truly courageous person.

Become aware of yourself as an individual of excellence, intelligence and skill. Take control of your life and create a self-image filled with energy and enthusiasm. Whether you're altruistically motivated to help people, or motivated by the desire to gain financial freedom in your life, when you think and act in a congruent way, you'll conquer barriers that have kept you from becoming a courageous, self-actualized and positive person. Your recipe for developing an image of success depends on substituting barriers of doubt, fear, guilt, negative beliefs, scepticism, and shame for healthier ingredients such as commitment, compassion, confidence, effective communication, emotional well-being, empathy, enthusiasm, laughter, love, physical and mental health, and passion.

Your success self-image consists of healthy feelings and behaviors needed to achieve your desires. Empowering beliefs and actions will keep you on the road to continual self-improvement. Awaken the happiness and joy that exist within you.

The courage to move forward, reach within your own depths, and develop a positive attitude and self-image, is the beginning of your open road to success. Hermann Hesse (1951) wrote in *Siddhartha,*

Within Siddhartha there slowly grew and ripened the knowledge of what wisdom really was and the goal of his long seeking. It was nothing but a preparation of the soul, a capacity, a secret art of thinking, feeling and breathing thoughts of unity at every moment of life.

The road to success is a never-ending path that leads to many valuable destinations. As a creative dancer, you create your own performance. You also create your own barriers and the ways to effectively overcome them. The dance never ends. It is a preparation for life.

Become the artist for your own life. With brush in hand, paint pictures of success for yourself and others. Just as your use of color can create passion and excitement, your use of words can do the same. Consistency in what you say and do is important because it eliminates barriers of pretense. As you eliminate the inconsistencies in your behaviors and beliefs, and eliminate the barriers of pretense in your life, your false self-image will disintegrate.

Remember, you're the author of your play and in charge of writing your life script. Use your pen to fill in the lines and spaces with positive ideas and successful statements.

Your script is made up of positive beliefs that reinforce your successes. The following statements will lead to success and will assist you in developing a healthy outlook.

"I know people care about me."
"I accept myself and others, unconditionally."
"I am a lovable and nurturing person."
"I am a valued and unique human being."
"The world is full of people who are basically accepting and positive."
"I will associate with positive people, and if things don't work out I'm free to move on."
"Hurt is a result of not understanding others."
"I can and will strive to make my dreams a reality."
"I will accomplish what I set out to do."
"I will get what I want and need in my life."
"I am in control of my life and my destiny."

Your enthusiastic affirmations, such as *I know things will work out as they are supposed to, I go with the flow, I take appropriate and positive action when necessary, I feel in touch with those I make contact with, and My faith is so strong that I can see how I attract and accumulate physical, emotional, mental, and spiritual wealth,* create win-win situations. When you take full control of your life and your feelings you create an attitude of success, develop courage, and feel, think, and speak in positive ways. Take these steps for living a richer and fuller life.

Overcoming Toxic Relationships

If your car takes high octane gasoline, would you put low octane in it? This will decrease your vehicle's performance. When you're driving down the highway and you come to a sign that says "Bridge Out/Road Closed/Flood Damage," do you continue down the same road until you're at a dead end? Or do you take an alternate route?

Knowing when to stay on the highway and when to change your direction is a decision you must make. Cutting corners, or taking the shortest route, doesn't necessarily mean your results will always be positive. Taking the "successful road" may mean you'll have to explore other ways to get to the same destination. It also means you'll be more prepared for obstacles when you see them coming.

Knowing when and where to make the right turn is like knowing when and how to change or maintain your relationships. Maintaining your speed (communication), accelerating while getting into the passing lane, or taking a different road can change your destination. Heading the wrong way in a relationship is just as disastrous as heading the wrong way on a one-way street. You may get into an accident.

Are you driving around in circles? Do you surround yourself with people who have critical or negative attitudes, and when you leave them you feel drained and dizzy? These are symptoms of a toxic, or venomous, relationship. Toxic situations appear to offer a sense of comradeship, but actually drain you emotionally and physically. Toxic relationships can be compared to a flood-damaged, or demolished, bridge. Once the relationship has terminated, you may continue on and hope that somehow it will eventually rebuild itself. However, extremely toxic situations, or people, may not change no matter what you do. They may need professional help.

When you do attempt to rebuild a damaged relationship, it will not

happen magically. Give yourself time. Whether it is building a bridge, or a relationship, eventually you have to make a strong commitment and connection to communicate. However, communicating in a toxic relationship can be like trying to send messages across the Grand Canyon without a vehicle for communication.

Communication is the vehicle that connects you with others. Healthy, positive communication brings you closer to others while unhealthy, negative communication can leave you further away. Certain relationships with your friends, family, or acquaintances, can be healthy or unhealthy. Given the alternative, would you live next to a toxic wastedump, or next to a field full of flowers and beautiful green trees? I believe many, if not all of us, would choose the field of flowers and trees. The decisions you make and who you associate with are very important to your psychological and emotional health.

• Equal versus Unequal Giving

Empathizing and caring for others is natural and important. However, taking care of everybody else first (especially their emotions), to the extent of your own detriment, can be extremely hazardous. Knowing when to support others, and when to let go, is a condition that requires the greatest courage.

The unequal relationship is selfish in nature. One person tries to interfere with, control, change, or improve upon another person for self-serving reasons. There are no benefits in the unequal relationship, only pain and fear. Discouragement, helplessness, self-blame, self-pity, and immobilization of self, are symptoms that individuals experience when involved in unequal relationships. These symptoms stifle and prevent people from developing self-responsible and self-directed behavior. Ultimately, feelings of inadequacy and self-pity emerge. The person may either ''give up'' or avoid changing, becoming despondent or angry.

The equal relationship is unselfish in nature. It creates a ''selfless'' attitude between two people. The selfless or equal relationship treats both individuals in an unconditional way, permitting each person to unfold, open-up and eliminate defenses or barriers. There is more expressiveness, independence, appreciation of separateness, love, and creativity in the equal relationship. In the equal relationship, you are able to express your feelings and thoughts without judgement. Communication is more satisfying and effective. There exists a mutual agreement to continually develop an attitude of acceptance and respect for each other. As Kahlil Gibran (1923) poetically reminds us in his book, *The Prophet,* "Love possesses not nor would it be possessed; For love is sufficient unto love" (p. 13).

Choose to form a healthy versus an unhealthy bond. Use the love within your heart as an energy source to awaken your consciousness and will. Direct your heart's energy with a selfless attitude to form healthy, equal relationships with others. Move forward and awaken your ability to demonstrate true love.

Constant Criticism is the second type of toxic relationship. Ask yourself, what motivates you to bond to a healthy or unhealthy person? Do the people you associate with constantly criticize every move and decision you make? Have you experienced situations when your ideas or decisions turned out positive, and yet others had to find something negative about them? In fact, there was probably a list of criticisms they were prepared to bombard you with. Choosing to stay in this unrewarding, negative relationship leads to frustration, self-disesteem, unhappiness, worry, and tension.

Fear of criticism means that you avoid criticism altogether just as you would avoid success. Certain kinds of constructive criticism can be positive and will help you correct any deficiencies. However, constant criticism is destructive and will drain you, destroying relationships. When you're continually being criticized you may create a shell, or armor, that blocks out all incoming information, including the positive.

When you constantly and needlessly criticize others, or you're the one being criticized, you run the risk of developing a sceptical attitude toward life. Unresolved scepticism may poison your perspective. Instead of developing an attitude of peace and prosperity, you may develop an attitude of misery and failure.

Healthy, successful relationships begin with your "will" or desire to have one. The healthier, more constructive relationship provides support and encouragement. There is less unconstructive criticism and more acceptance of others. You are excited to help others learn more about the positive aspects of life, and you pay attention to positive characteristics of their strengths. When you focus on the person's strengths, versus their weaknesses, you build their self-esteem and confidence, and help them to develop their full potential.

Decide to overcome the discouragement and disappointment associated with constant criticism. Believe that you have the determination, purpose, and the desire to attain your goals and dreams. If one plan fails replace it with another and keep going. Turn defeat into victory by continually rebuilding your plans. When others constantly criticize you to change, without offering you positive alternatives or suggestions as to how to change, decide your own course of action. Maintain unwavering courage and self-control. Your courage, self-discipline, and effort to persist in sound, intelligent undertakings will be rewarded.

Accepting an Inferior Position in a relationship that causes you undeserved pain and frustration is a third kind of toxic relationship. When you're involved with others do you feel like you're walking on eggshells? Are you concerned with how you walk, and when and where to stop? Have you landed in a minefield, or relationship, filled with so many potentially explosive communications that you spend your time continually defusing each one? You probably don't drive a tank so your protection is limited. You can be wounded by flying objects caused by explosive communications.

Attempting to get out of an inferior position in a relationship is similar to removing shrapnel from your skin. It's painful. You have to ask yourself, what were some of your unconscious motives for getting into this position to begin with? Sometimes it's important to remember a painful experience from a time when you did take a risk and involved yourself with someone, but something backfired. Confronting the pain associated with this 'backfire' is essential to overcome it. At the time the pain may have seemed too unbearable. You were motivated to avoid the pain. Taking a mental detour temporarily alleviated the pain, anger and frustration. However, assuming an inferior position and avoiding others caused you more pain and frustration in the long run. Removing the painful event by avoiding the unpleasant situation, or taking an inferior position in the relationship, seemed logical at the time. After all, your partner could "take care" of you. However, this also backfired because you resented being "taken care of."

Ask yourself, how much time and energy do you invest in allowing yourself to stay in the inferior position? What purpose does it serve?

If you believe that staying in the inferior position in your relationship gives you a degree of control over your "superior" partner, then you're sabotaging yourself. Being in an inferior position serves no purpose because there is no reciprocity, no give and take. It is a contradiction in terms because when you believe you are inferior, you usually act in inferior ways. Nonreciprocating relationships cause pain. Attempting to block or channel the pain you are experiencing to someone or something other than yourself is self-defeating. The pain returns and results in further confusion because you may give yourself mixed messages. "Although I'm inferior I have control over the situation." "Then why do I need to be inferior?"

Blocking and redirecting pain, even though the pain is still present, confuses the signals you give to your body. You may have to first admit that a painful feeling exists in order to conquer it. Trying to convince yourself that you no longer feel the sensation of pain only magnifies the problem. Suppressing your feelings is as dangerous as over-reacting to them. Confronting your feelings, and the people you want to share them with, is your first step in overcoming pain and increasing reciprocating communications. Failure to do so maintains the cycle of pain and increases negative, nonreciprocating communication. Toxic relationships and negative communication threaten and detour satisfaction of your healthy needs. If someone offers you a bomb of pain, anger, unhappiness, or confusion, you can refuse the bomb.

How long will it take to change your negative communication and attitude within this kind of unhealthy relationship? It depends on the degree of resentment you've accumulated. Resentments are like shrapnel. They can be razor sharp. Communication, based on resentment, can penetrate the emotional and psychological skin of the person on the receiving end. Obviously, the more resentments you have toward others, the longer it will take to change negative communication and attitudes into positive ones. When you remove resentful, negative communication from your interactions with others, you can begin the process of healing.

Once you decide to let go of being in an inferior position, assume responsibility for your decision and follow through with it. When you take a risk, and something positive happens as a result of taking the risk, don't sabotage yourself. Don't let past pain or guilt immobilize you and your success. Allowing pain and guilt to uncenter your peace of mind is like hitting a major pothole and not doing anything to correct it. This can cause a misalignment and throw you and your vehicle out of balance. You'll probably have to realign and balance the wheels and front-end.

The same goes for toxic and unhealthy relationships. After getting out of the hole, or the unhealthy relationship, you have to realign your mental, emotional and physical state. The bumps, or unevenness in the road, may not disappear altogether in your relationships. However, you've begun the process of becoming more aware and skilled at negotiating them. The amount of time you wait until you realign and balance yourself depends on you.

Don't wait to change a highly negative, unhealthy or toxic situation. If you drive your car when it's out of balance, you feel the wavering effects when you attempt to stay on the highway or turn the corner. It takes more energy and concentration to maneuver your vehicle. It's the same with relationships. Do not allow others to sap you of your energy and strength. Get out of the potholes in your life that make you unhappy and unhealthy. Align yourself. Lift yourself out of your inferior position. Remove the shrapnel of negative communication and attitude before it infects the rest of your physical and mental health. Tell yourself, ''Disease is unacceptable, under no circumstances will I allow unhealthy attitudes, or people, to infect me.''

Eleanor Roosevelt made a great observation, ''Nobody can make you feel inferior without your consent.'' Stop allowing others to bring you down and throw you out of balance. You can eliminate unwarranted conflict and frustration when you persevere and develop an optimistic attitude.

• Perseverance: The Key to Overcoming Barriers

Perseverance implies continuing to do something in spite of obstacles. Swimmers have great endurance, or perseverance, especially when attempting to set a new record. Mountain climbers and weight lifters push themselves to the limit when increasing their stamina. Students forge new pathways in education as they expand their awareness and move into undiscovered territory. Entrepreneurs rise above the mundane and set new limits in the social and business world.

You, too, have pushed yourself at one time or another especially when you were told to ''give up.'' What is that deep desire within you that prompts you to hold on? It's your faith and belief that you can persevere in spite of all odds.

Perseverance is the driving and staying power of ''will.'' It musters all your strength and energy and directs you toward your goal.

Toxic relationships and *negative communications* are barriers to growth. The pain and anger caused by toxic relationships is like an emotionally fused land mine which can go off at any time. When this land mine (or person) explodes, toxic reactions cause internal storms or upheavals affecting your physical and psychological stability. Once you cultivate and develop perseverance, you can continue in spite of toxic and negative communications that cause pain. When negative thoughts and words penetrate your attitude, it's like listening to a program that keeps telling you how you're going to fail, rather than succeed. Negative thoughts or unhealthy suggestions from others fill your mind, both conscious and unconscious, with psychological messages that lower self-esteem. Negative thoughts or unhealthy suggestions from others also affect your body with physiological responses that can endanger your health.

Perseverance is key in helping you steer your way through negative and toxic feelings. Perseverance is the fuel that motivates you to courageously sweep over these land mines to detect and defuse them. Don't allow the poison in these venomous relationships to affect you. The greater your self-esteem, the stronger your tolerance in dealing with negative situations. As you create more peak experiences and positive moments in your life, the greater will be your ability to persevere. Develop the will-power and desire to control your own destiny.

There are five personal factors that will help you to develop perseverance.

1. Develop the sense of being in control of your life. Remember, You have control over your destiny!
2. Develop a network of friends or family to provide "social support." A supportive alliance with a select few will help you carry your plans through to fruition.
3. Develop personality factors such as hopefulness and flexibility. Eliminate all negative influences and persons in your life. You have the ability to change your situation and your attitude!
4. Develop will-power and a definite purpose. Continually move forward with your plans, dreams and aspirations.
5. Decide I Can I Will.

Start taking action, now, by establishing healthy relationships. Changing negative communications and relationships into positive ones will help you overcome insurmountable barriers; and it will help you live longer. A study conducted at Johns Hopkins found that one of the strongest prognosticators of cancer, mental illness, and suicide, was 'lack of closeness to parents' and a negative attitude toward family. Negatives do more damage than merely causing pain.

If someone hurts you, do you have to try to get them to love you? Do you shoulder their pain and take responsibility for them instead of letting them take responsibility for themselves? What do you have to gain by accepting another person's pain? Stop setting yourself up in an inferior, no-win situation. Relationships and situations that force you to assume complete responsibility for others are detrimental to your health.

Once you decide that your attempt at changing a negative relationship into a positive one is taxing you beyond your limits, stop trying and eliminate it altogether. Your first responsibility is to balance and coordinate your mental, emotional and physical stability. Allowing yourself to remain in an inferior position, and accepting less instead of more, greatly affects your perseverance. When you decide to emphasize the positive aspects of yourself you begin to:

1. Increase your endurance and positive momentum.
2. Accept responsibility for yourself and no one else.
3. Become more self-reliant.
4. Replace unhealthy, dysfunctional relationships with healthy ones.
5. Trust your intuition and feelings.

Encouraging, positive relationships filled with healthy communications help you to recognize and defuse emotional landmines. Let go of pain and unhappiness. Take responsibility and speak up for yourself. When you take responsibility for your own emotions, actions, and thoughts, you take responsibility for your life.

• Planning Your Road Map to Personal Success

Planning for success is an important way to overcome barriers to growth. It's similar to taking a vacation. You need a guide, or roadmap, to keep you on course and give you direction. Would you attempt to navigate a ship on the open sea without a chart or map? Of course not. Even the ancient mariners used the stars and constellations to find their way.

A plan is a powerful tool for achievement. It's a magic key that helps you reach your goals and gives you the momentum to get through difficult passageways. Planning prevents unnecessary detouring, and helps you take responsibility for your actions. In Hermann Hesse's (1970) *Narcissus and Goldmund,* the monk Goldmund asks Narcissus, "What is your goal?"

Narcissus responds, "My goal is this: always to put myself in the place in which I am best able to serve, wherever my gifts and qualities find the best soil, the widest field of action. There is no other goal." Goals are what keep you going and give you your focus. Keep focusing on your goals and continually take the needed steps to reach them. Your ability to keep moving after achieving one goal depends on how clearly you see the next step to set new goals. There are six ways to focus on your goals and plan your success. It is important to include the following in your goal-setting procedure:

1. Identify your goal and make it a realistic one. You must care about it.
2. Select a goal that you can work on, rather than something someone else has selected for you.
3. Make sure it's specific, not vague. For example, choose a skill like "Communicating more effectively with your friends by using positive vocabulary," or "Managing your time more efficiently by stating a time and date for getting your goal accomplished." Selecting a goal you can do something about gives you the power and influence to actively and assertively accomplish your goal.
4. Have at least one goal or objective every day. Feel a sense of joy and fulfillment whenever you take a step toward accomplishing your goal, or objective.
5. Experience how your feelings and thoughts are pulled by your stated goals.
6. Reward yourself for goal, or objective, accomplishment. Remember to be consistent when rewarding yourself.

Goal-setting is an ongoing, reciprocal process between you and the world. Accomplishing your goals helps you to overcome inner barriers of fear, and affirms your self-confidence. Rollo May (1969) believes, "It is self-affirmation that gives the staying capacity and depth to one's power to be."

Goal-setting is not a mundane process. It generates out of your human need for self-drive and accomplishment. This drive for accomplishment is innate, it comes from within you. When you set goals, it solidifies you physically, mentally and emotionally. You begin to feel more connected to yourself and to the world. This also implies a 'we-ness,' a bond that unites people—an empathetic tie and capacity to identify with others who are accomplished.

When you are willing to set goals, your motivation becomes more defined and less confused in everyday interactions. Setting goals and designing your dreams and aspirations is a commitment to participate in a dynamic relationship and interaction between yourself and others. Committing yourself to be in a relationship with others helps to create an environment of self-support. The "willingness" to define your goals and aspirations provide you with the motivation to focus on achieving your goals.

Your "will" to take action and achieve your goals is different than wishing your goals to complete themselves. Wishing is a desire for the possibility of some act or state arbitrarily occurring. When it comes to making your goals happen, wishing can be self-sabotaging. "Willing" is self-responsible behavior. When you take conscious control of your life, you actively plan your course or direction. Determining your direction builds positive momentum in your life. Creating positive momentum and enthusiasm drive you to share your enthusiasm with others. When you encourage others to believe in themselves you build positive momentum in their lives.

Your first responsibility as an encouraging person is to yourself. Make your best effort to provide the proper atmosphere for growth to occur. Discovering your own personal power and "free will" requires an attitude of positive self-control. Lewis Losoncy (1977) states that the encouraging person makes a commitment, "A commitment to help the self-defeating person view life differently, take personal responsibility for his/her effort, evaluate this effort, and develop self-rewarding and self-encouraging skills" (p. 85).

Without commitment, you are helplessly determined by others and their "will." To overcome fear and determine your own destiny, you must make a commitment to believe in your own *"free will."* By being committed, you actively assert yourself in your relationship with others and the world. When you become self-supportive, you become better equipped to overcome barriers that prevent you from reaching your goals. By committing yourself to your goals, you generate power in taking a risk to achieve your goals. Rollo May states, "Exercising the will . . . is really effort of attention, the strain in willing is the effort to keep the consciousness clear, a strain of keeping the attention focused." Developing "clarity of focus" increases your self-determination and your ability to make up your own mind.

Remember the elephant's strength and large size. As a young elephant, the trainer put a chain around his leg, and it was staked to the ground. No matter how the elephant tugged at the chain, he could not move but a few feet. When he became an adult, the elephant still believed that he could not roam freely because of the chain clasped around his leg. You, too, may have had that same conditioning— conditioning that did not allow you to expand to your full potential. Are you conditioned to accept a predictable and stable situation that will make you feel at ease? What happens when you're in a situation that requires you to change your attitude and possibly experience some discomfort? What do you have to do to break your inner chains?

Breaking the shackles of past behaviors and attitudes that have kept you from growing and changing can be uncomfortable. Change is not always comfortable, and it's definitely not stable or predictable. Deciding to make new, positive changes that generate excitement, or to remain in your stable, sedentary world (or relationship), is a decision only you can make. You have one question to ask yourself: What's rewarding to you? If you're comfortable with staying in one spot in life, that's your choice. But if you want to move on and travel to new destinations, mentally and emotionally, then go for the change.

The challenge is to take conscious control of producing positive thoughts and behaviors that will create healthy choices for you and your life. Make up your mind and overcome your fears. Your positive attitude, like your *"will,"* is powerful medicine. Turn on your power key to success and become more dynamic. Get fired up and drive with conviction toward your dreams.

• A New Vista is a New Life

Personal growth and self-awareness are like vitamins that help you regulate your physiological and psychological functioning. This growth process is essential in building inner strength and physical stamina. It requires you to commit to changing your limiting beliefs and emotions. Changing negative behaviors into positive ones to successfully communicate with others does not happen accidentally. You must create a mental and physical strategy to overcome previously formed barriers and detours set up by yourself and others.

Are you 'mentally rehearsing' how unsuccessful you're becoming by saying, "Why trouble myself? Nothing will come of it, I'm not getting anywhere. I'm the kind of person who has difficulty making decisions." When you focus on negative statements you begin to feel negative and you get negative results. Don't sabotage yourself and your success. Negative feelings are barriers that prevent you from making positive choices to change and grow. Remember Alice in Wonderland when she's standing at the crossroads confused as to which road to take. She then asks the Cheshire cat which road to take, and the cat responds, "Well, where is it that you would like to go?" Alice responds, "I don't know." The cat then says, "Well, if you don't know where you'd like to go, it doesn't matter which road you take" (paraphrased from Alice in Wonderland).

Ask yourself, are you standing on the crossroads trying to figure out which road to take? One road is labeled positive communication and beliefs, and the other one is labeled negative communications and beliefs. Now is the time to decide to use your energies to develop positive strategies to overcome self-sabotaging thoughts and behaviors. Overcome your negative communications and tear down the walls that you've set up for yourself. Take the positive road!

You can change negative beliefs into more positive ones by practicing the following statements.

I will do my best.

I am responsible for my purpose and goals in life.

I have the right to be me, not influenced by behaviors, attitudes, and beliefs that are not mine.

I have the power to change and become an independent, fully-functioning person.

It is my right to become the person I want to be.

I am in the process of creating a more enhanced self-image.

I am more self-determined.

Construct your road to success by removing the barriers and obstructions that get in your way. Take this opportunity to compose positive statements that will change your counterproductive beliefs and attitudes.

_____

_____

What actions can you now take to change your positive beliefs into constructive action? Develop an action plan to change an aspect about your life. Be realistic and specific. Give yourself a time line to complete each action. What can and will you do to:

Increase Your Self-esteem and Self-confidence:

Action I: Time Line:

_____   _____

_____   _____

_____   _____

_____

Action II: Time Line:

_____   _____

_____   _____

_____   _____

_____

Action III: Time Line:

_____   _____

_____   _____

_____   _____

_____

I Can I Will

Increase Your Self-respect:

Action I: Time Line:

_____   _____

_____   _____

_____   _____

_____

Action II: Time Line:

_____   _____

_____   _____

_____   _____

_____

Action III: Time Line:

_____   _____

_____   _____

_____   _____

_____

Empower Yourself:

Action I: Time Line:

_____   _____

_____   _____

_____   _____

_____

Action II: Time Line:

_____   _____

_____   _____

_____   _____

_____

Action III: Time Line:

_____   _____

_____   _____

_____   _____

_____

Redefine Your Diet, Body Weight, and Physical Fitness:

Action I: Time Line:

_____   _____

_____   _____

_____   _____

_____

Action II: Time Line:

_____   _____

_____   _____

_____   _____

_____

Action III: Time Line:

_____   _____

_____   _____

_____   _____

_____

Removing the barriers that have created negative attitudes and beliefs unchains you from past conditioning and guilt. Experience the freedom that exists within you. It is your right, your life and your destiny.

Your willingness to take positive action will make you stronger. Learn from your experiences. Now get ready to ascend from the valley and climb new peaks. Explore and experience life's new vistas and horizons.

• Shift into Third Gear

''Even when walking in a party of no more than three, I can always be certain of learning from those I am with. There will be good qualities that I can select for imitation, and bad ones that will teach me what requires correction in myself.''

CONFUCIUS

Whether you select good qualities for imitation, or make corrections within yourself, you are increasing your ability to change your thoughts and feelings. The way you perceive things, mentally and emotionally, determines the way you look at life. Integrating your self-image and personality helps you to develop inner strength. Utilize your resources to facilitate your own growth.

When you begin to integrate your inner and outer-image, you must first listen to and become aware of your own movements, posture, thoughts, and feelings. When you affirm yourself, you facilitate your personal growth and increase your self-confidence. Having a sense of direction and knowing where you're headed assists you in taking action to achieve future goals.

May the road you choose safely guide you toward your destination. However, whether the road is safe or unstable, your inner security and positive self-image will help you overcome detours and barriers along the way. Your inner strength and self-esteem empower you to overcome resistance. Changing negative attitudes and expectations into positive ones will condition you for success. *Overcome Barriers to Change!* Call on your inner strength and determination and forge your own way!

5.
Overcoming Resistance to Growth

Success is failure turned inside out—
The silver tint of the clouds of doubt—
And you can never tell how close you are,
It may be near when it seems afar.
So stick to the fight when you're hardest hit—
It's when things seem worst that you mustn't quit.

—ANONYMOUS

Choice and Decision Making were making their way up a steep path when Choice said, "How do you truly let go of resistance?" Decision Making walked over to a huge pine tree laying on the ground and rested on its trunk. A red-tailed hawk circled overhead. He then responded, "The practice of letting go comes through the practice of not allowing oneself to become attached to the outcome. When you're not attached to the outcome, you have nothing to let go of."

Choice and Decision Making, finding themselves on the crossroads, realized that they would allow their feelings and intuitions guide them along the path of truth, the road to success.

"Decision Making," Choice continued, "Perhaps our total self, the synergy produced by our mind and body, is wiser than our mind alone.''

''Yes,'' Decision Making remarked, ''We can become more accurate in our intuitions and overcome our resistances when we feel whole and complete in ourselves. When we are one and the same, and exist in the present, the here and now, at rest in a moment of time, we are at peace.''

What kinds of situations have you experienced that you feel blocked your growth and change? Did the situation make you feel like you were stuck in mud or quicksand? Choosing to get stuck in uncomfortable experiences may be one way of avoiding change. Avoiding change is a resistance to growth. It's like stopping at a red light and refusing to notice when it turns green. How long will you wait before you make a move? Do you sit and analyze yourself or the situation while others drive around you? Or are you too cautious, unable to make a choice to go forward, to stop, or change direction? Proceeding with too much caution slows you down and prevents you from experiencing the positive side of change.

Growth and change are healthy functions of every human being. When your personal growth and ability to change are blocked for some reason, you may experience more resistance in dealing with new situations and people. It's not easy to adjust and remain flexible to external changes if you're not able to make changes within yourself.

Imagine swimming past the breakers in the ocean and as you swim toward shore you get caught in a riptide. The resistance you experience swimming against the current will only carry you further out to sea. You need to swim parallel to the shore around the riptide current, letting go of your resistance, and then you'll be able to swim towards the shore with ease. You have to remain flexible and improvise so you're not working against the current, or yourself.

Whether you are attempting to grow in your relationships, or changing the way you communicate, ultimately, you are responsible for overcoming your resistance. Believing that your environment is totally responsible for making you the way you are today is only an excuse when situations arise that demand change and improvement. When you perceive you are unable to do something because you were criticized in the past, you create an excuse not to grow and change today, or in the future. When you overcome resistance to growth, situations that demand decision-making become a challenge especially when your goal is self-improvement.

When you believe your environment is totally responsible for your behavior, you give up personal freedom and choice. Sitting on a mountain and waiting for the sun to rise in the west can be frustrating especially if you're resistant to facing east. If you're resistant to taking action because of past conditioning, you need to realize that it's time to develop a new set of behaviors and a new game plan. Changing habits can be difficult because in some way they are safe in their familiarity. It can be exciting to break a habit and change your direction.

The salmon overcomes resistance during its journey swimming upstream to the spawning grounds. The salmon's purpose is to use its strength to swim upstream, against the current, to reach the spawning pools to ensure the continuity of its species.

Sometimes reaching a goal requires moving against the current with persistence, endurance and purpose to overcome resistance to growth.

When a stop light hasn't turned green for ten minutes, you can change your strategy and move in a direction that will get you to your destination with more ease.

The other extreme is making a decision to accelerate and move forward without first looking both ways or not stopping at all for red lights. This can be dangerous especially when you're in the middle of an intersection. Continually living in dangerous situations is a resistance to growth of awareness. When you resist growth, you may be avoiding assuming responsibility for yourself. It may be difficult confronting feelings that cause us to experience emotions such as anger, fear or pain. However, it is important to recognize which emotions are unproductive, or irrational, to take the first step in overcoming or changing them into productive ones.

Taking responsibility for your life and learning how to balance situations and emotions will help you appreciate the benefits of positive growth and change. You create and determine your actions, beliefs, and emotions.

Explain how overcoming your resistances by taking action and breaking familiar patterns can allow you to experience the positive side of growth.

_____

_____

_____

How does this add to your appreciation of life?

_____

_____

_____

There are times in the growth process when you come to a plateau. Different kinds of plateaus are there for a reason.

The action state of change and growth requires a surge of energy from the *body* and *mind*. This places the individual in states of equilibrium and disequilibrium. Rest and rejuvenation are essential to the growth process. The body requires the appropriate nutrients or it will not function efficiently. Plateaus allow for the assimilation of change. You can see the next mountain peak from your position on the plateau.

A race car cannot remain in the fast lane without taking a pit stop to change oil, tires and refuel. The driver has to prepare the vehicle for the remaining laps so he and the car won't burn out. Just as a stop sign prevents you from darting out into an area with a high flow of traffic, or a "no swimming/dangerous undertow" sign prevents you from getting into dangerous waters, signals from others can prevent you from disclosing in a relationship. Stopping and reasoning can facilitate your growth and is especially helpful when you're experiencing unusual discomfort. You don't have to burn out.

What kinds of external behaviors from others prevent you from moving ahead in a relationship? (Example: harsh vocal tone, harassment)

What kinds of external behaviors from others move you ahead in a relationship? (Example: smiles, positive tone of voice, eye contact, affectionate touch)

When you stop yourself from moving forward, your reasons may be unknown to you at the present moment. You may be experiencing behaviors from others, or internal signals from within, that tell you to stop and reevaluate the situation. Unconscious motivations such as wanting approval and direction from others, or desiring companionship because it fulfills certain needs and boosts your self-esteem, can communicate your reasons for hesitating or moving forward in relationships.

Unexpressed anger, blaming yourself or others, giving yourself or others mixed messages, failure to accept reality and realize alternatives, and conditional acceptance are resistances that can prevent you from growing. Finding new ways to overcome and let go of these resistances is essential for personal growth and success.

• Unexpressed Anger

Unexpressed anger is an example of a self-imposed stop. When unexpressed anger is out of proportion to the situation or issue at hand, it can cause an emotional blockage or illness. When you stop expressing yourself emotionally, you create an inner resistance that blocks the natural flow and development of your identity. One needs to make contact with their unexpressed feelings and deal with them head-on to overcome them. If you need to climb several steps before entering into a museum to see an art exhibit, or climb a mountain to reach the top and experience elation, the best place to start is by taking the first step and keep moving forward.

Imagine yourself walking in a river against the flow of the rushing water. Experience the water's powerful force as it rushes toward you. The water's powerful force hinders and opposes your movement forward, just as the repression of unexpressed anger opposes your movement forward in the healthy growth and development of your identity. Unexpressed anger creates an inner resistance that blocks and discourages your growth and change. Letting go of anger through proactive expression and forgiveness will release all emotional, mental and spiritual blockages.

What kind of inner resistance (internal emotions) stops you from expressing yourself? (Example: feelings of doubt, fear, caution, stress/distress, etc.)

_____

_____

_____

Becoming aware of the resistances that block your developing identity is the first step in overcoming them. The second step is to eliminate them. Eliminating resistances means you *must* and *will* face nonconstructive beliefs and emotions to prevent you from being overwhelmed. *Recognize* the emotions that you have control over and choose behaviors that will create new actions to immediately reduce and eliminate undesired feelings. Three, *objectify* issues and concerns. *Gaining* support and encouragement from significant others will strengthen your commitment to overcome resistance to growth. Four, *communicate* to yourself, and others, with honesty and integrity. *Reawakening* your true feelings empowers you to take action to nurture yourself and do the things that promote self-esteem. Positive self-esteem will strengthen you to confront emotional issues that discourage or overwhelm you. You *Can and Will* overcome feelings of self-defeat and discouragement when your confidence is high.

There are people that will blow their horn or shout out car windows at you while you're deciding which way to turn. They'll also attempt to set you off course by putting obstacles in your way, like refusing to move into another lane to let you pass (especially when the coast is clear). These *"progress blockers"* know how to push your *"anger button."* How long do you allow them to manipulate your emotions, and how long do you have to accept it?

You can remove and overcome inner resistances, and change negative situations into positive ones, by expressing your feelings in a positive way. *"Please allow me to finish my statement without interrupting me"* is an example of a positive, verbal expression of anger or frustration. When you release nonproductive feelings, there's more room to express yourself and discover your healthy, productive emotions.

What ways can you positively express some pent-up anger or frustration?

_____

_____

_____

Continual physical exercise (e.g., going for a long walk, climbing a mountain, hiking in nature, working out in the gym, cross-training) can reduce and permanently eliminate unnecessary tension and anger. Pay attention to actions that make you feel healthy and positive.

What positive, physical ways can you reduce and eliminate anger?

_____

_____

_____

An adverse, or uncomfortable, situation can become an opportunity for you to make a positive change. Have you ever been in a situation, or experienced a certain feeling, that at the time seemed unbearable to you? However, as you dealt with the feeling, or situation, you were able to turn your adversity into an opportunity for success. Turning an adverse, unfortunate situation into an opportunity for success means taking action by voicing your opinion and standing up for what you believe in.

Turning a negative, losing situation into a positive, winning one takes practice. For example, a car dealership loans you a rental car, and tells you that there's no cost. When you return the car, they tell you that there is a cost. You can say, "I understand that there is a miscommunication, and I apppreciate your position. However, the original agreement (of a no-cost rental) remains in effect, and next time I'm sure you'll double check before signing the agreement. Thank You, and I look forward to doing business here in the future." There's no guarantee how the other person will respond. However, what really matters is your accepting responsibility for your own choice and decision-making.

Taking the proactive approach and taking responsibility for your feelings help you realize that the situation is a positive learning experience. Take responsibility for your own personal change. Make a commitment to improve yourself on a continual basis. When you do, positive life changes will move you to a new level of awareness. Continually see your adverse situations as a challenge and opportunity to overcome them, not as a block or deterrent to growth. Your resistance to growth becomes less and less as you face your adverse condition, or feeling, without anger and hostility. Once you eliminate anger, you can clearly visualize how to change negative beliefs and situations into positive ones.

Focus on encouraging yourself. When you're encouraged and optimistic, you see alternate ways of viewing your life. Experiencing your own unique balance and center is a movement from stagnation to change and growth. Courageously accepting yourself, unconditionally, means thinking your own thoughts while accepting responsibility for all your alternatives. Your desire for achievement and acceptance is motivated by the expectations you have of yourself. Self-acceptance and positive self-expectation create your attitude of optimism. Realize that your courage and strength motivate you to reach your goals and become a self-confident person.

Describe how you can turn an adverse situation into an opportunity for success. Take a proactive approach! You can do it!

_____

_____

_____

When you react to a situation by blocking your feelings, there is very little opportunity for growth and change. If you continue to take action that makes you unhappy, keeps you in a rut, or you know will never fulfill you, then you're blocking your awareness and accepting a disadvantageous outcome. Turn your disadvantages into advantages by using your time and energies to change your negative habits and thoughts into ones filled with commitment, creativity, excitement, and joy.

What one habit or thought can you change, right now, to trigger an empowering emotion that will produce excitement, optimism and joy?

This one change is a step forward that will contribute to your continual growth, change and success. When you consistently change the quality of your life, you'll influence and help others change the quality of their lives as well.

• Selflessness vs. Selfishness

Choice asked Decision Making, "Do you agree that processing information through the mind and heart is one way of letting go of unhealthy, past experiences?"

"Yes," replied Decision Making, "And it's also how you let go of anger. False bonds, or communication, without true commitment mean nothing."

Decision Making continued speaking while Choice watched a family of hummingbirds hovering above the trees and mountain boulders near a stream, "The wedding band does not mean anything by the weight of its gold or the diamonds it contains. The wise person knows that one must give in order to receive. The things of the material world will not fulfill the desires of your heart."

"Decision Making," asked Choice, "How, then, does selflessness show truth in relationship? Indeed, how does selfishness become poison to growth?"

Decision Making paused, then replied, "Once there was a great Sheik who invited the whole village to his daughter's wedding feast.

With great anticipation, everyone prepared themselves for the great feast which was to begin at high noon. A beautiful ritual of the wedding was for the bride and groom to exchange crowns of silver and gold. As the two merged the flames of their individual candles to light a third, singular one, the symbolic flames of the two became one, and bells sounded. All cheered and the wedding feast began. As the two kissed, grain was thrown over the bride and groom to insure fertility."

Choice was intensely listening as Decision Making continued, "Late after sunset, the Sheik gave out white wedding cakes to each and every guest as they left the feast contented on the best of food and drink. Past the torches of the gate, a guest stopped and bit into the white, wedding cake. Inside was a gold coin. All the guests broke open their cakes and looked upon the coin of gold. Then, the first guest who opened his cake spoke out loud, 'What a cheap Sheik,' he sounded, 'he only gave us one gold coin.' "

Instead of complaining about what you don't have, cultivate and appreciate what you do have. Cultivating your attitude so you become a positive person, and appreciating who you are based on your strengths, will create a positive outcome. Your road to success depends on the choices and decisions you make. Deciding what to say when you discover the contents of your "white cake" can make you feel excited, uneasy, challenged, or cautious. Your task is to see the situation from a 'selfless' perspective rather than a selfish one. Accept responsibility for your actions. If you feel your actions produce negative results, and the outcome is unacceptable, then change your actions.

> When you allow yourself the freedom to change,
> you also allow yourself the freedom to grow and
> discover new roads to success.

Remember a time or a situation when you faced a moderate degree of challenge. You may have noticed a distinct change in your feelings. As the time drew closer to achieving whatever it was you set out to accomplish, you felt more alive and more aware of your surroundings. Your aliveness and vitality produce pleasurable feelings and is self-encouraging. Your perspective and emotions reach new peaks and plateaus as you choose your direction with conviction. Mountain climbers look for the next spot to place their feet, race car drivers look for their next best opening to move ahead in the race.

When one door, or opportunity, closes another one opens. The opportunity for challenge helps you to grow, change, and take charge of yourself. Working towards a new and exciting goal, or eliminating a disempowering emotion or habit, empowers you to control your present situation and your life. As your ability to develop a new perspective increases, you put yourself in the driver's seat to greater self-empowerment.

Face it, there are people in this world that enjoy agitating you. Maybe it's because they lack direction in life, and attempt to communicate their frustration to you by pushing your 'anger button'. They may feel that they have no other way to relieve their pain but to cause you pain. If they resist communicating with you in a positive way, let go of the situation. Give yourself a time frame to decide how long you'll put up with their manipulative behavior. There's no reason to let unwarranted conflict or pain affect your life. Speaking up for yourself is your choice and decision.

Anger and agitation with others will slow you down and block your progress toward success. Making a move to slow down, speed up, or get out of their way by changing your direction, is a positive step forward. Whether your challenge or adversity be facing the situation (or person) or letting go of it, taking action is your opportunity for change and success. Your ability to master your emotions depends on the positive decisions you make. Creating a life of personal fulfillment is based on your inner strength, determination and communication. *You won't know where you're going until you start heading in that direction.* Direct yourself in the direction that provides maximum enjoyment and positive interactions with others!

• Blaming Yourself or Blaming Others

Self-blame and blaming others are resistances that block your success. Blame, like fear and doubt, drains your energy and prevents you from moving ahead and facing challenges. One reason why people do not grow, move ahead, make changes in their lives, or take responsibility is because they blame themselves for falling short of reaching a valued goal. Relationship disharmony, career dissatisfaction, and family conflict are a few examples of *symptoms* which can result from unfulfilled goals. Taking responsibility for those actions you do take, rather than blaming yourself for inaction, is one way to create opportunities for growth and fulfill your goals.

When you take personal responsibility for your thoughts and actions, you act courageously and are not immobilized. When you act on your greatest dream, whether it's achieving status as a great sports figure, participating in the Olympic games, becoming a hero or heroine like NASA's courageous astronauts, graduating from college, becoming a successful entrepreneur, doctor, or dynamic speaker, or loving others with optimum emotional impact, take action. Overcome the curse of inaction by thrusting yourself forward. Become an active participant in determining the outcome of your own life.

Depending too heavily on others for self-support is a resistance that sabotages your taking action. Self-sabotaging beliefs and emotions limit you from taking risks and prevent you from learning how to grow and change. If you have difficulty taking action then you not only blame yourself, but blame others, especially when situations don't conform to your expectations. Self-blame results in self-pity while personal responsibility results in action and change.

A person who lacks self-esteem and needs support from others is lacking the essential qualities that promote survival self-support. Frederick Perls (1980) suggested that when the individual is frozen in an outmoded way of acting, he is less capable of meeting any of his survival needs, including his social needs. Blaming others, and not accepting responsibility for your action, is a resistance to change and a form of denial. Statements such as, "If only it weren't for ——, my life would be great," and "If only it weren't for ——, then I could go to Europe" are examples of blaming behavior.

Your manipulations of self-blame and blaming others are directed towards preserving and cherishing your handicaps rather than getting rid of them. Lewis Losoncy (1980) states, "Self-blamers put the blame for their behavior on themselves as opposed to holding themselves responsible. When people take the blame for their behavior, this is just as unproductive as placing the blame on external factors" (p. 14). Self-blamers are filled with blame, guilt, worry, shame, and doubt. They use all their energies blaming themselves and have no energies left to get out of their self-created ruts.

How do you reject positive ideas about yourself? List a few here. Example: Negative self-talk.

—————————————————————————

—————————————————————————

—————————————————————————

How do you prevent yourself from changing habitual or negative patterns in your life? What are some of the specific behaviors? Example: When I get upset I keep my feelings to myself and don't let the other person know that I'm upset.

—————————————————————————

—————————————————————————

—————————————————————————

It's your ability and belief in yourself that will determine your success! If you see yourself in a negative way and believe you cannot succeed, you will not. You can change the way you look, feel, and act in life. Each self-image statement will either limit or facilitate your potential success. As long as you believe you are restricted, you create your own resistances and no growth will occur. As long as you believe a certain task will be impossible, it will be impossible.

When you have positive beliefs in your own ability, you live up to your own expectations. Your positive expectations create a reality that can and will influence your success. Your self-esteem, self-confidence, and self-respect, are strengths that empower you to change your self-image. Using positive self-talk and behaving in a way that eliminates counterproductive actions reduce inner resistance and increase your strength.

Your self-worth is confirmed when you're able to relate to others and be acknowledged in ways that you value. Your road to success is determined by the choices and decisions you make. Success is not a haphazard, unplanned event. Success can be measured by the degree you learn how to achieve managing your mental, emotional, physical, financial, and spiritual life.

Stop blaming yourself, or others, for your lack of initiative. ''Blaming behavior'' is another resistance that blocks your personal change and allows you to give up your personal power. As a result, you stall yourself and hope that success comes to you. In Eugen Herrigel's (1971) book, *Zen in the Art of Archery,* the Zen Master says to his student: "Do you know why you cannot wait for the right shot and why you get out of breath before it has come? The right shot at the right moment does not come because you do not let go of yourself. You do not wait for fulfillment, but brace yourself for failure. So long as that is so, you have no choice but to call forth something yourself that ought to happen independently of you, and so long as you call it forth your hand will not open in the right way— like the hand of a child. Your hand does not burst open like the skin of a ripe fruit" (p. 50).

Become more aware and open to the stream of life flowing within you. Overcome resistance by taking responsibility for your life and your destiny. Become responsible for everything you feel, think, and do. Focus your energies in the direction where you feel fulfilled. Neglecting parts of your personality by not acknowledging what makes you feel joy, or by failing to believe in yourself, will block your fulfillment and success. Allow yourself the opportunity to experience joy and success while developing your individuality.

Stop stalling for success. Change your negative behaviors that have restricted you from living a healthy, happy and productive life. Start conditioning yourself, both physically and mentally, and change your limiting behaviors and emotions into productive, positive action.

> Waiting for the right condition to arrive is like sitting in
> your car and waiting for it to start without turning the key.

Put your personal key in the "ignition of life" and turn yourself on! Realize that *you expand your options as a result of your decisions.* Ask yourself: *how* do I achieve my goals, and *what* actions do I need to take to achieve them. Stating your questions in the manner just mentioned is key in reaching your successful destination. When you decide to spend your energy growing in new directions, rather than defending unproductive behaviors, you break the chains of past conditioning. When you shift responsibility for your feelings to others, you avoid your responsibilities and feelings. Your decisions are yours and not the responsibility of anyone else.

When you resist taking responsibility for your decisions, or for making changes in your relationships with others (especially when changes are needed), you put yourself on hold or stand-by. When an operator puts you on hold, how long will you wait? Probably not more than three minutes, then you hang up and try again. Why then do you hold on to relationships that are unsatisfying or even punishing? If the person's signal is toxic, you've got two choices. One, hang up and try again until your signal and their signal get clear. If you add humor or positive feelings to the situation and the conversation remains toxic, then it may be time for option two. Hang up and don't call back. There's only so much you can do.

Holding on to unsatisfying relationships and listening to others without getting involved are like calling someone and holding on while they're busy talking to someone else, or talking at you. Frustrating yourself reduces your willingness to stand up for what you believe in.

Overcoming your resistance to change by speaking up for what you believe in is the first step in the change process. The second step is to appreciate and learn to use your special strengths such as being altruistic, nurturing, kind-hearted, strategizing, achieving, self-dependent, assertive, directing, organizing, flexible, and a unifying force for others.

These two steps will help you accomplish your goals. Remember, take the initiative and speak up for yourself. And when you find the coin of gold, it's your choice as to whether or not you complain about what you don't have or appreciate what you do have.

• Giving Yourself or Others Mixed Messages

Have you ever experienced a time when the car traveling in front of you gave a left hand signal but moved into the right lane? How did the situation make you feel? Confused, angry? What did you experience? Frustration?

How would a football team ever score a touchdown if the quarterback tells the tight end to move to the left side of the field along the forty-yard line, but passes to a running back on the opposite side of the field on the thirty-yard line? If this was your strategy, how successful would you be at making a touchdown, or reaching your goal? You must clarify where you're going so you, or others, won't end up somewhere else.

Giving mixed signals to friends and family, telling them you're going one place only to end up somewhere else, is a resistance to understanding your behavior. The assumption is that you're not responsible for determining the outcome for your actions.

How often do you confuse yourself, or others, by saying one thing but doing something totally different? What don't you accomplish by giving mixed messages? List some examples:

_____

_____

_____

Another kind of mixed message is when your actions contradict your posture and tone of voice. Giving yourself mixed messages prevents you from experiencing positive feelings or situations when they do occur. The implicit, or unconscious, message is that you don't deserve happiness or success.

Sabotaging your own success, by giving yourself and others mixed messages, may be your way of avoiding the pain of failure or the fear of success. Don't undermine yourself by giving yourself a mixed message. Empower yourself to accept positive feelings when they do occur. Experience immediate sensations of pleasure as you increase positive feelings and thoughts.

What could you say to yourself when positive feelings and thoughts do occur? Make a list.

_____

_____

_____

You only frustrate and discourage yourself when you resist changing your negative self-talk. When you resist taking risks, or experiencing something new and challenging, it's usually because the unfamiliar is frightening to you or because you fear failure. When you're confronted with situations that are unfamiliar to you, think about ways that will help you energize your courage.

For example, when you meet someone for the first time do you feel uneasy? Change your fear into empowering emotions and thoughts, and develop successful communication, by making contact with your new acquaintance! Believe you're able to accomplish your goals. When you experience a breakthrough in learning how to communicate with others, celebrate each success! Remember, each positive self-image statement creates unlimited potential for success.

You can change this inaccurate observation (i.e., believing that you're unable to connect with new people) and change your conclusions by taking action to free yourself from discomfort and embarrassment. Building your road to success by exchanging self-defeating self-talk for a new vocabulary of success is your first step. The second step is to congratulate yourself each time you believe you can connect with new positive people. The third step is to reward yourself when you follow through with your new belief and make positive contact with another human being.

Overcome your resistance to grow by changing your "failure program" (self-defeating self-talk) into one of success. What is an example of a thought or action that kept you chained to inaccurate observations and feelings of self-defeat?

Example: I tried photography for a while but I could never bring any attention to my pictures. No one seemed to care so why should I continue?

_____

_____

_____

Now, change your limiting thoughts or actions to ones which will help you energize your courage and help you overcome your fear of failure. Feel free to release yourself from unreasonable demands, doubts and self-defeating behaviors.

Example: "I'll keep taking photographs, and with practice and educational classes I'll succeed and capture the moment. I will strive to make each picture a masterpiece. Each person has their own unique style, and I have mine."

One way to awaken your inner power and strength is to eliminate the "I could never" statements from your thoughts and vocabulary. Changing your thoughts from what you "can't do" to what you "can do" will help change a negative self-image into a positive one. Continually reinforcing yourself by creating positive thoughts instead of negative ones will assist you to develop beliefs and behaviors that you desire.

A friend of mine worked in the personnel department of a large hospital. She told me a story of a woman whom she thought the world of; however, this person was rated as a junior clerk and at the bottom of the pay scale. The woman often complained about her salary and felt she could accomplish more. One day an opportunity arose in which a senior clerk was leaving the medical record department. My friend called this woman aside and gave her advance notice so that when the job was posted she could apply for it. This would mean a raise in salary and advancement.

The woman, however, did not apply for this job nor the several other positions that arose over the next six months. Instead of appreciating the opportunity being given to her, the junior clerk went to her superior and complained that my friend was harrassing her. My friend was criticised for taking interest in this woman and for trying to help her achieve and advance.

Sometimes when people are in a rut, they have a difficult time climbing out of their rut. The junior clerk avoided acting in her own best interest. In fact, she shirked the responsibility for her own life and situation while blaming my friend for acting in her best interest.

The truth is, no one can ever fulfill you except you. One way to fulfill yourself is to stop demanding appreciation, fulfillment, and a sense of completeness through others. Unreasonable demands and self-defeating behaviors create resistance in communicating with others. If I were to continually make demands of you without appreciating you for who you are and what you say, you're going to either react with anger, or withdraw by becoming defensive and avoid contact.

Second, to overcome your resistance to growth stop downplaying another's good intentions especially when you ask for them. This is not only discouraging but it will also create uncomfortable and hurt feelings in your relationships with others. Thank the person for their suggestions whether you use them or not.

Third, stop sending mixed messages. Failure to do this creates confusion and in the long run is harmful to everyone. Practice your communication skills by giving congruent (straightforward) rather than incongruent (mixed) messages. The way to eliminate unproductive behaviors and overcome resistance to growth is to develop characteristics such as:

• *Realism:* to perceive reality accurately and fully, and accept yourself for who you are.

• *Spontaneity:* Having no need to put up a pretense or wear a mask. Exhibit openness and flexibility to change.

• *Problem-centered vs. ego-centered:* Be concerned and sensitive to solving problems and finding solutions. Stop focusing on a ''what's in it for me'' attitude. Focus more on a ''what's in it for us'' attitude. When we share our concerns and work on the problem together, we will accomplish our goals.

• *Autonomy:* Being able to set your own goals and values rather than depending solely on the opinions of others. Invite yourself to become successful!

• *Ethical Sensitivity:* Become aware of the ethical implications of your actions. Realize that your actions affect not only one person, but many. Use foresight and speak with integrity when interacting with others.

• *Openness to Experience:* Enjoy the uniqueness of each experience and every encounter from a positive perspective. Overcome the curse of inaction by challenging yourself to take new, exciting risks. Develop positive self-talk. Experience ecstasy and awe, wonder and excitement. Feel strengthened by your daily experiences. These six characteristics will help you develop a strong, positive attitude.

Changing unproductive behaviors and communications will help you eliminate resistance to growth. What action or communication can you now change to eliminate unproductive behaviors that prevent you from growing?

Example: ''I have the power to choose what I want to think about and the power to choose where I will direct my attention.''

Your attitude, like your "will," is powerful medicine. A strong, positive attitude is the antidote that will help you change your negative communication and behavior.

Take responsibility for your personal success! If you only have the winds of passion in your sails, it will blow you all over the ocean without direction. With only the rudder of reason, you'll then be able to navigate your vessel and point yourself in the right direction, but not go anywhere. To develop a strong, positive attitude and overcome resistances, you'll need both the winds of passion and the rudder of reason to arrive at your destination. As the philosopher Goethe suggested, "But for a person in a given situation to accomplish anything, he must stick to one definite point, and not dissipate his forces in many directions." You have the power to control the direction of your thoughts and emotions, and the power to choose where you will direct your attention!

• Failure to Accept Reality and Realize Alternatives

I've listened to many people say, "I could never speak to a group of people. To be in the spotlight on stage, and know everyone is waiting to hear what I have to say, is frightening." This is a reflection of the person's self-image. Although this self-image statement may be false, the person acts as if it were a true statement. If you act on what you believe is true, your beliefs back you up. Believe you can't speak in front of a group and you won't. Believe you can't go to college, be successful, or change your destiny, and you won't. It depends on how you interpret reality.

There are five basic mistakes individuals make when interpreting reality:

1. Overgeneralizations: "There is no fairness in the world."
2. False assumptions or impossible goals: "I must please everyone if I'm to be loved."
3. Misperceptions of life and life's demands: "Life is so very difficult for me."

4. Denial of one's basic worth: "I'm basically stupid, so why would anyone want anything to do with me?"

5. Faulty values: "Get to the top regardless of who gets hurt in the process."

These negative, preconceived beliefs are examples of self-defeating, self-sabotaging thoughts that create resistance toward your change and growth.

Do you have any negative, preconceived beliefs similar to the ones mentioned above that create inner resistance and sabotage your success? List them here.

Example: "I'm the kind of person who can't open up new accounts or influence people to see the benefits of my product. I'll never succeed."

_____

_____

_____

Additional research (Adler, 1939; Losoncy, 1969) suggests that much discouragement and failure to move ahead and take action are the results of two errors:

1. Failing to face and accept reality as it is; and,

2. Failing to realize all the possible alternatives still available when the reality is faced.

Once you face and accept reality, you can then move forward with your alternate plan of action. You have control over your own personal interpretation of reality. Becoming aware of all your alternatives and options gives you the personal freedom to change your mind. When you change your discouraging beliefs, you alter your self-defeating feelings. Remember, you control your feelings and beliefs. Believing that you have the power to change your own reality will change the actions you take!

Take this opportunity to change some of your discouraging beliefs and alter your self-defeating feelings. Example: "I can and will succeed at influencing people to see the benefits in my product (or service). And I'll smile and feel great while communicating to them."

A positive change in your feelings and beliefs encourages you to interpret your personal reality in a positive way. Change your beliefs and you change your behavior, change your behavior and you change your beliefs. Sir Issac Newton believed, "To every action there is an equal and opposite reaction." This formula holds true for your beliefs, emotions and behaviors.

Have you ever noticed that when you change your beliefs about something that matters to you—achieving peak physical condition, creating new relationships, eating healthier food, managing your emotions, increasing the power of your mind, becoming more positive, etc., your behavior starts to change. In fact, you begin to act in a more positive way. And likewise, when you change your behavior, and start taking action to become physically fit and emotionally and mentally more positive, your beliefs about who you are and what you can accomplish start changing in a more up-beat, enthusiastic way. Sir Issac Newton was right, it works both ways.

A change in your outer image will influence a change in your inner image and vice versa! Coco Chanel said, "If a woman is poorly dressed you notice her dress, and if she's impeccably dressed you notice the woman." Looking like a winner, fashionable, always appropriate, feeling confident and assured, and achieving optimal physical condition, health and vitality, will encourage you to climb out of your rut and overcome resistance. You can transform and change your personal interpretation of reality.

Remember, developing self-confidence and self-esteem and becoming motivated means that you change your outer image as well as your inner image. Changing your reality and becoming positive may be tough, but with work, perseverance, determination and concentration you will succeed. Decide to make the change!

How can you change your viewpoint, feelings, or your behavior to reflect your new, positive personal reality?

_____

_____

_____

Developing a positive personal reality will create a balanced, productive and fulfilling lifestyle.

• Conditional Acceptance

Love, acceptance and approval are the most powerful reinforcers a human being can experience. When an individual has an attitude of partial approval or partial acceptance of others, an attitude of conditional acceptance develops. Statements such as, ''I'll accept you when . . . ,'' create hurt, anger, fear, and distrust. When you attach unreasonable conditions within a relationship, your opportunities for accomplishment and enjoyment diminish. An attitude of conditional acceptance creates resistance to healthy communication with others.

When you go to a restaurant and order a full-course dinner are you satisfied with a partial meal when you ordered a complete dinner? Of course not. Settling for being partially accepted as a person is not enough because it doesn't provide enough emotional and physical nourishment. Conditional acceptance hinders your self-respect and creates resistance toward growth and change. If I allow myself to be partially accepted as a person, or accept others only on a conditional basis, this reduces the trust and comfort needed to achieve effective communication.

There's no need to place a limit on the amount of love and energy you give or receive. You don't have to settle for being accepted as a partial person. How often have you heard the statement, ''She/he has a great body?'' Don't let anyone reduce you to a bunch of parts—hair, nails, skin, arms, or legs. What about the person's other qualities, such as being competent, cooperative, conscientious, genuine, honest, faithful, forgiving, judicious, noble, persistent, sensitive, spirited, straightforward, well-adjusted, thoughtful . . . to only mention a few? When you're not appreciated as a whole human being, you become discouraged and your self-esteem and confidence suffer.

Start accepting and confirming yourself as a total physical, emotional, mental, and spiritual person. Start behaving and believing that you are unique, a "crown of creation." When you expect more of yourself you'll get more! When you communicate through a negative self-image your message lacks confidence and determination. Conditional acceptance breeds mistrust, fear, and rejection. This condition also creates damaging self-talk, decreasing self-esteem and producing nonharmonious relationships.

Fritz Perls (1969) believed that when a person is lacking the support of 'self-esteem' and is in constant need of external support, the person's energy is drained and has no surplus for integration and self-organizing. The discouraged, conditionally accepted person is lacking the essential qualities that promote survival self-support. A person who has low self-esteem may experience low motivation. The person who feels conditionally accepted may immobilize him/herself with handicaps, becoming disempowered instead of taking responsibility for his/her life.

Overcoming resistance is difficult when one is discouraged and demotivated. Taking risks is not a high priority for the person who experiences conditional acceptance. When the person is disheartened and discouraged they may say, "Why trouble myself with anything? With my luck I was bound to fail. I'm not getting anywhere." These statements are signs of frustration and hopelessness. Conditional acceptance creates discouragement and resistance toward change and growth. Unconditional acceptance creates encouragement, warmth, and understanding in relationships. Resistance to growth is eliminated when one is unconditionally accepted.

Unconditional acceptance, "I'll accept you as you are," facilitates trust, joy, acceptance, and success thus increasing self-esteem and effective communication. Developing unconditional acceptance for others is important because it creates a relationship of respect, vitality, and healthy interpersonal communication. When you accept others for who they are, unconditionally (with no strings attached), you become an encouraging and empowering influence, helping to develop positive self-esteem. Empowering actions and beliefs help you overcome handicaps and resistance to growth.

When a person experiences unconditional acceptance, they feel respected and valued. Unconditional acceptance is nonthreatening thus allowing the person the freedom to choose and decide for him/herself. Whereas conditional acceptance focuses on the person's failures, unconditional acceptance focuses on the person's successes. Harvey

Mackay (1990) writes, "What coaches understand is that no matter what the lesson is, you can teach it only by instilling a sense of pride, not shame in the pupil."

When you provide others with hope and a relationship of trust, support, acceptance, and optimism, they will discover that their motivation, momentum, and support come from within. *When you help build and empower the person to use relationships for growth and change, you increase their self-esteem.* Overcoming resistance to growth is essential to communicate with confidence and heal emotional and psychological wounds. Keep communication channels open. When you help the people around you, that's when you grow the most.

Unconditional acceptance positively changes your sensitivity to and acceptance of others. Developing harmonious relationships through unconditional acceptance encourages you to become more caring, compassionate, and consistent in your actions. Your courage to develop unconditional acceptance is your most valuable resource for creating successful relationships. Winston Churchill noted, "Courage is rightly esteemed the first of all human qualities because courage is the quality that guarantees all other qualities." The courage to continually improve yourself guarantees your passion and commitment for lifelong success and personal fulfillment.

• Overcoming Self-Sabotaging Behaviors

Changing long, established behavior patterns is as difficult as recognizing and understanding them. Self-sabotaging behaviors prevent you from conditioning yourself for success.

How, then, can you eliminate sabotaging beliefs and emotions? First, understand and accept yourself before attempting to understand and accept others. You have to take a journey within for personal evaluation. This means looking inside yourself and listening to your inner dialogue or self-talk. Remain open-minded to what you see and hear when understanding your beliefs. This is essential when making constructive changes in your behaviors. Deciding how far and deep you want to go before introspection is your decision. However, you can take your life to a new level when you discover empowering insights to eliminate damaging self-talk and undermining behaviors.

The poet W.B. Yeats noted, "Why should we honor those who die on the field of battle, for a man may show as reckless a courage in entering into the abyss of himself." Initially, growth and change may feel uncomfortable and unsettling. However, in the long run, you'll find that it's the best choice of any other alternative.

Deciding to let go of self-sabotaging behaviors that prevent you from changing takes courage and a personal commitment to develop more effective actions. Before you go around believing you can change the beliefs and behavior of others, you have to first change yourself. This means overcoming resistances and sabotaging behaviors that have prevented you from experiencing an optimistic attitude. No matter what obstacles you face, developing an optimistic attitude, and changing unrewarding behaviors and beliefs, will awaken you to eliminate self-sabotaging behaviors.

What specific actions can you now take to become aware of and overcome your sabotaging beliefs and self-defeating emotions?

1. Recognize that you are at the crossroads where your decisions and choices are yours and yours alone!

2. Realize that you're the one making the conscious decision to change your damaging self-talk and undermining beliefs and behaviors. No one else can do it for you.

3. Change "I can't" or "I won't" to "I Can I Will" on a consistent basis. Pay attention to the emotional changes going on within you. Be prepared to physically describe your changes and write them down (in a journal). Repeat the process of writing down your changing feelings and behaviors and compare your notes every day. Measure your progress by the visible reoccurrences of positive self-talk and healthy behaviors. Continual negative self-talk will create resentments and disempowering beliefs. Self-resentment is the seed that grows into self-sabotaging behaviors.

4. Plant the seeds that produce positive, empowering beliefs and actions. Ask yourself, "Are my actions linked to pleasure-producing situations or to pain-producing situations?" Take the road that gives you pleasure, not grief. The personal growth experienced from facing a fearful or painful event, or adversity, is important for self-improvement. However, don't make a steady diet of it. You can grow and change by cultivating positive emotions such as joy, excitement, and happiness.

5. Understand your own motivations. Your motivation for recognition, self-respect, love, acceptance, and financial success are equally rewarding and create personal fulfillment. Accept your-

self and appreciate the choices you make every day. Your positive perspective and commitment to take charge of your actions, beliefs, and emotions will motivate you along your path of success.

6. Believe that you can "will" yourself to take action to overcome self-sabotaging behaviors. You can transform and change your unproductive beliefs and behavior when you use encouraging language, such as: I will choose to . . . , I will plan to . . . , I will become . . . , and I will . . . (fill in the blanks with healthy verbs and adjectives).

_____

_____

_____

Continually creating and using empowering messages such as, *"I Can and I Will succeed,"* *"I Can and I Will produce healthy, harmonious beliefs and behaviors"* will make you realize that you actively choose your own alternatives in life. When you become more self-determined, accepting and more responsible, you experience the freedom to choose alternatives that will move you forward in overcoming self-sabotaging behaviors. Empowering messages create the inner strength and determination to remove self-sabotaging thoughts and beliefs from consciousness.

Believe in destiny, and believe that your decisions spring from your inner depths, your "will" to succeed. You determine your destiny just as you create the path that brings you toward self-fulfillment.

Trusting yourself to make the decision to overcome your self-sabotaging behaviors is a courageous event. It demands that you take personal responsibility for yourself. Becoming self-responsible assists you in overcoming your resistance to growth. Move forward on your path to success. Use the knowledge from your past experiences to make a conscious decision to change your behavior and communication. Begin to explore the core of your inner self. Decide to take positive action and overcome resistance and obstacles to growth.

Now you have the best of both worlds. Believing that you have the power and option to move forward in overcoming your self-sabotaging behaviors will give you the freedom to choose your own destiny. Making decisions based on empowering messages from within yourself prevents you from driving the wrong way down a one-way street, or reaching a dead-end in a personal or professional relationship.

Carl Rogers (1961) noted that when the individual comes to feel that his evaluation of himself lies within, "Less and less does he look to others for approval or disapproval, for standards to live by, for decisions and choices. He recognizes that it rests within himself to choose and that the only question which matters is, 'Am I living in a way which is deeply satisfying to me, and which truly expresses me?' The individual who is thus deeply and courageously thinking his own thoughts, becoming his own uniqueness, responsibly choosing himself, may be fortunate in having hundreds of objective outer alternatives from which to choose...but his freedom exists regardless" (p. 52).

To live in a way that is deeply satisfying for you is to begin your journey into *selfhood*. Your personal journey into *selfhood* is called *individuation*, a process whereby you establish your identity as a self-determining person. Your self-determination empowers and enables you to overcome resistance. *Self-determining individuals* use their inner strengths and resources to create healthy beliefs, behaviors, and emotions to experience life's abundance.

When you're self-confident, you accept yourself, and others, unconditionally. Your self-confidence and self-determination assist you in finding the right mental and emotional balance to create truly productive and successful relationships. These precious resources help you overcome resistance to growth to ensure your development of positive self-esteem.

As you move along your road to success you're more fully able to respect and trust yourself, becoming more responsible for your decisions and your life. Becoming aware of, and sensitive to, your inner feelings, and the feelings of others, is a movement toward personal fulfillment and maturity. When you understand that maturity is accepting others for who they are, and accepting yourself for who you are, you're able to overcome resistances to growth.

Begin now and develop your attitude of complete acceptance. This new awareness of unconditional acceptance facilitates a dynamic process through which we *awaken* and *affirm* ourselves, giving new meaning to our relationships with others.

Creating positive perceptions and empowering beliefs establishes a strong foundation for overcoming self-sabotaging behaviors and resistances that prevent you from finding the right mental and physical balance. *Take charge of your own growth and development!* Becoming more self-aware, self-confident, self-determining, and sincere energizes you to *Overcome Resistance to Growth.*

6.
Open Road to Success

The golden glow on the trees and mountains reflected the sun's final sigh of the day. The bright star highlighted the mountains on the new moon when Decision Making suddenly appeared on the dry, dirt road amidst sage brush, manzanita and pine. The scent of pine and sage permeated the air.

Choice called out as he walked toward Decision Making, "I thought that was you walking on the road as I rounded the curve. You blended into the landscape so well I couldn't tell."

As twilight filled the valley, Choice turned to Decision Making and asked in a concerned tone, "What does the future hold in store for us?"

Decision Making's eyes were fixed on the moon and stars when he turned to Choice and responded, "The only thing for certain is that the future is uncertain. Remember, there are no guarantees. The path on which we've already tread is behind us. The important thing is to resist getting stuck in a rut, focus on the 'here and now,' and move forward with positive momentum on the path to success."

Decision Making continued, "Once there was a large, well-known zoo that desired a white Siberian tiger for one of its exhibits. They commissioned an experienced trapper who knew where white Siberian tigers roamed and hunted for food. The trapper flew his plane to a remote area, and waited patiently amidst the mountains of ice until a cub suddenly appeared without its mother. The trapper caged the black-striped, furry white young cub and flew it back to the zoo. The white cub walked around its 'new home' with hesitation. Time passed and the cub became an adult. Spectators loved to watch the white Siberian tigress as she walked around the exhibit and growled in her penetrating voice. However, the walking area within the exhibit was only twenty-feet in length. The tigress would pace without any substantial changes in her walking pattern.''

Decision Making continued, ''Six years later it was decided that it was time to take the rare Siberian tigress back to her natural home in the land of ice and snow. They caged the tigress and flew her back. When they arrived, the trapper lifted the cage door and waited for the tigress to freely roam in her natural environment after the release.''

Decision Making looked at Choice and said, ''What happened?''

Choice responded, *''One must find their natural instincts to survive and succeed.''*

Getting Back on Track

Have you ever found yourself in a rut? What do you need to *awaken your instincts* and get out of the rut? How do you change counterproductive behaviors and habitual patterns in a way that will help you to succeed?

When you're entrapped, what can you do to free yourself and change your unrewarded course of action? You can confront your situation head-on, or analyze and plan an escape route to free yourself and reach your destination. Reaching your destination and committing yourself to new alternatives requiring risk challenges you to face your fears.

Taking action and risking new movement will get you out of your rut. Facing the fear of adventuring into the unknown requires courage. Obligations to others such as mortgages, car payments, and job demands, things that give you a false sense of security, may have put you in the rut. Stepping out of the rut means courageously changing certain circumstances that have dictated your direction. Getting yourself back on track is the first step toward success. Driving on new streets, avenues and in new surroundings allows you to experience freedom from ''rut behavior.'' Leave your ruts behind!

On the road to success, your perception of reality must be positive. Negative perceptions and attitudes place roadblocks in your way that prevent you from changing life patterns. You will find difficulty and resistance when the purpose of your change is unclear. Resistance to change increases when you're not sure which way to go or which road to take. Examples of statements that show overcoming resistance to change are, "Things are not really so bad, I'm convinced that I can make a positive change by improving the quality of my thoughts," "I can change destructive habits by progressively achieving goals that increase the quality of my life," "I am becoming more effective and challenged in working on my interpersonal relationships," "I can and will make an effort to change my counterproductive behaviors," "When I set my mind to it, I can find enough reasons to accomplish my goals," and "Changing my behaviors and taking positive action will help me to succeed in finding a way to accomplish my goals in the present, so my future will be exciting and bright."

Each self-image statement either limits or facilitates your potential success. What can you do about changing a self-defeating statement, and when will you do it? What would be a good first step? Remember, focus on your strengths and resources.

Now, what are some statements that can get you on the road to success?

_____

_____

_____

_____

Make a plan and put these positive statements into action.

_____

_____

_____

_____

The self-image changes what you can or cannot become. Then influencing, or changing, your self-image determines which direction you take in life. Do you stay in your self-created rut or jump on the bandwagon of success? Accepting yourself for who you are will establish healthy behaviors and will help you change your discouraging beliefs. Making positive changes in your feelings and behaviors motivates you to become more self-accepting and more consistent in your actions.

When you are prepared psychologically to change your beliefs, you'll go beyond your *"perceived limits."* You will be able to change yourself. When you make a change, make it for the better. One way to overcome resistance and make a change is to be precise about what it is that you want to change, and then decide to take action to make the change.

Reaching your destination is accomplished by the actions you take during the journey. When you focus on the process and highlight your positive moments, you increase your inner strength which causes you to become a dynamic person—a winner.

Accept yourself, and devote your intelligence and energy to becoming self-supportive and motivated. Experience all of life's peaks and plateaus. As you begin to travel on your journey keep in mind, *you can and will succeed.*

Choice and Decision Making sat in a large, concrete hall listening, in silence, to the Dalai Lama. Choice whispered to Decision Making, "You only have so much time on this planet, above the ground. Appreciate the simple life, why complicate things?"

Before Decision Making had the chance to speak, the Dalai Lama said, "Give of yourself, altruistically."

Decision Making turned to Choice and said, "What then does it take to become an enlightened, benevolent person?" Choice was about to respond when the Dalai Lama said, "Remember, whatever you want to accomplish, a little bit at a time."

Choice turned and looked into Decision Making's eyes and said, "The goal then is to learn how to progressively let go of your resistance and move forward in life by integrating all your inner and outer resources. There's no shortcut on the path of success. For one to grow one must learn to *let go of negativity.* Material things may bring you temporary happiness, but peace of mind and good health is everything. While you are walking on the path, there needs to be spiritual growth and discernment. Without spirit, one is an empty vessel on the path. Our mission is to *continually nurture our spirit and foster spiritual growth and awareness in others as well.*"

A presence was felt—Love.

• Overcoming Resistance: The Key is Optimism

Optimism is your main resource for overcoming resistance. Optimism is like a magic potion that transforms the way you think, act, and feel. It changes your entire physiology and psychology, and is the catalyst that helps you overcome resistance to change. When you're optimistic, the belief in your own ability is so strong that obstacles are turned into challenges to be dealt with or mastered, and conquered when necessary. The belief that "you have everything to gain" is an attitude that gives you the strength to believe in yourself, and overcome pessimistic beliefs from others.

Optimism is a resource that impacts every aspect of your existence. It's an inner light that shines throughout your being. J. Krishnamurti summed up optimism in a nutshell when he said, "In oneself lies the whole world and if you know how to look and learn, then the door is there and the key is in your hand. Nobody on earth can give you either the key or the door to open, except yourself." Focus on developing your assets, courage and strength. You have the power and the will to develop and uncover your own resources.

Use your key as a *power tool* to understand which experiences, or situations, contribute to your success. And which experiences, or situations, detract from your becoming successful. When others attempt to detour you away from success, it's usually because they're stuck in a rut. Have there been times when others discouraged you, wanting you to believe that what you were doing was not worthwhile? This is perhaps one way of wanting you to take responsibility for their lack of success or misery. They may not be aware of their self-sabotaging behaviors and self-defeating vocabulary. Projecting their pessimism on you, and wanting you to take responsibility for their lack of success, will only temporarily alleviate their pain.

Remember a time when you came up with a new idea and someone discouraged you? Rising above the initial discouragement wasn't easy because feelings of pessimism from others dominated your thoughts. Since you probably have had similar, demotivating experiences you can relate to another person's pessimistic attitude. However, this is not enough reason to let their pessimistic attitude, or pain, affect you. *You can reinforce yourself by restating that you still believe in your ideas.* You don't have to shoulder the responsibilities, or accept the negative habits, of others. Your number one priority is to reinforce your empowering beliefs and positive attitude. Becoming more responsible means becoming more responsive and empathetic, not reactive. Share your positive beliefs and feelings of success with others. Listen for the emotional response of their reply. Empathize with them and suggest ways for self-improvement.

Influential role models have a great influence on how and what you believe. Whether they be teachers, parents, friends, actors/actresses, managers, great sports figures, or spiritual guides, role models can (1) motivate you by generating enthusiasm and a positive mental attitude, or (2) demotivate you by unjustly criticizing you. Discouraged, demotivated individuals assume they are inadequate, without self-worth and self-esteem. Positive or negative ideas and thoughts about who you are can influence and determine your behavior. Role models can either accentuate the positives or negatives. Choose to focus on positive role models!

Your motivation for love and esteem in your personal and social life help you to make emotionally satisfying choices.

When you're emotionally satisfied, you seek love and esteem because it strengthens your relationships with others. When you're not able to make emotionally satisfying choices, your relationships may be based on liabilities and detriments rather than on strengths and assets. Making positive changes in your relationships increases your self-confidence. A change in your self-confidence will give you the courage to make changes in your self-image. Changing the way you look and feel changes the way you act.

A positive self-image helps you to accept responsibility for overcoming resistance to growth. Ultimately, you're responsible for yourself and for overcoming your resistances. Overcoming resistance to growth with a positive self-image generates encouragement and optimism. Generate optimism in others by using positive language and by showing concern. You have the choice to overcome discouraging beliefs and communication. Like the mythical Phoenix rising from the ashes to be reborn, *you must also rise from the ashes of despair and pessimism and breathe in the life-giving energy of optimism.*

Becoming more responsive means focusing on finding ways to increase the positives, in yourself, and in others. Before you can change counterproductive feelings and behaviors into more productive ones, you must first understand, trust and accept yourself. Krishnamurti (1954) clearly stated, "To transform the world, we must begin with ourselves: and what is important in beginning with ourselves is the intention. The intention must be to understand ourselves." The next step is to willingly communicate empathy, encouragement, optimism, trust, and understanding to others. Conveying these positive attributes to others will create rewarding relationships.

Challenge yourself to pay attention to your feelings and your behavior. Remember, your success is linked to a positive self-image. Athletes are taught how to train their minds to increase their performance. As you increase your performance, and your effectiveness in relationships, you empower yourself to increase your physical and psychological instincts and potential. When you find yourself unwilling to do something, perhaps you are giving yourself a mixed message which blocks realization of your goals and your dreams.

What defensive barriers, or negative communications, block your goals and dreams? Where does your self-rejection or unwillingness to change originate? Whether this unwillingness comes from role models, or from some insecurity within yourself, actively change counterproductive feelings and behaviors by communicating in a congruent, trusting and sincere way. When you *highlight the positives* in the process of communication, you pull down any defensive barriers. As barriers and resistances are removed, you can then "get through" to others and change your ways of relating. One way to help others change their negative beliefs and way of relating is by modeling positive behavior and communication. When your way of relating is straightforward, you communicate sincerity to others, and to yourself. Modeling the right actions can influence others to change their attitude and perspective in a positive way.

Modeling negative actions and behaviors can influence others to change their attitude and perspective in a negative way. When you distort your beliefs, you develop logical errors to back up these beliefs. Prescott Lecky (1945) believed that people fail to succeed not because they are incapable of success, but because of their failure self-image.

Lecky noted that negative preconceived beliefs and expectations build up resistances and convince people ahead of time that it would be impossible for them, with their limited capacities to succeed.

Remember, to overcome sabotaging behaviors and beliefs, one must *increase their desire* and *change their motivation* to create the quality of life they envision for themselves. One must take conscious control of their mental, emotional, physical, and spiritual direction. Rollo May, the noted psychoanalyst, wrote "Courage is not the absence of despair, it is rather the capacity to move ahead in spite of despair." In times of despair, your inner courage will move you forward to overcome your pain, changing sabotaging beliefs and behaviors. Develop the courage and conviction to move through your despair and pain. You can manage your emotions and accelerate your growth by increasing your courage and enthusiasm.

Developing high-spirited interactions with others is yet another way to erase sabotaging beliefs and emotions in yourself, and others. This is accomplished through the life-giving force of encouragement. Lewis Losoncy (1980) wrote, "Encouragement is the process whereby one focuses the individual's resources in order to build that person's self-esteem, self-confidence and feelings of worth . . . Encouragement involves focusing on any resource which can be turned into an asset or strength" (p. 65).

Dr. Losoncy (1977) goes on to say, "The encouraging person rewards any effort on the part of discouraged persons to change. Any effort made represents a success. The effort, however minute, is a sign of growth or 'coming back to life'. You as an encouraging person must be there at this valuable moment" (p. 120). You must make clear to the discouraged person that effort is the most important resource they possess.

How is this accomplished? First, *positively influence* the individual's beliefs and expectations, creating a self-fulfilling prophecy of success. Second, *compliment* and *reward* others by using positive vocabulary when they show initiative and effort. Third, *reinforce* them when they achieve their goals. And four, *affirm* them as someone special. As an encouraging person, your first responsibility is to make your best effort in providing the proper atmosphere for personal growth to occur.

Encouraged persons are optimistic. They are motivated by growth because their positive self-image and self-esteem supports them.

Encouraged persons accept responsibility for who they are, and what they strive to become. Relationships with others are based on facilitating effective communication to produce a change in the discouraged person's behavior.

Encouragers help others in becoming more self-determining, self-supporting, active, responsible, and self-disciplined. As an encourager, believe you have control over your own decisions and choices. Encouragers determine their own direction, and positively influence the direction of others, on the road to success.

Fear, on the other hand, is a great discourager. Encouragers will not allow the fear of being ridiculed to influence expression of their new ideas. They know that it is essential to overcome fear because it drains their creative resources of time and energy, and can distort their perception. Fear can be experienced in many forms, among them, (1) fear of emotions, (2) fear of disapproval from others, and (3) fear of spontaneity.

Encouragement and *optimism* are the antidotes to fear. Committing yourself to using the uplifting power of encouragement and optimism will energize your creativity to produce the success you deserve. *Optimism and encouragement create the fuel that supercharges your internal engine to operate more efficiently while increasing your power.* These two motivational forces produce a positive attitude with which to create peak performance, improve your self-image, transform your limiting beliefs, improve your communication skills, and create unlimited success and happiness.

• Discernment

In Hermann Hesse's *Demian* (1970), Emil Sinclair questioned, "I wanted only to try to live in accord with the promptings which came from my true self, why was that so very difficult?" Why would it be so difficult to live in harmony with your true self? Changing your self-image so that you are congruent and in harmony with your beliefs and actions is one of the most challenging events you will ever undertake. It will also become the most fulfilling. When your actions, beliefs, and feelings are in balance, you live in harmony with your inner voice, your self-image.

Discernment, harmony and balance are the building blocks that help create your foundation for an optimistic attitude. When you sharpen your perception, you clearly recognize that your optimism is like a precious jewel—priceless—helping you to overcome most, if not all, of the resistances that prevent you from changing and living life superabundantly. Self-defeating and self-sabotaging thoughts and emotions are resistances that block your spontaneity and independence. They are the barriers that detour you in your quest for self-reliance and success.

Your optimistic attitude—I Can I Will—opens your road to success by exploring new beliefs and ideas that generate positive self-growth. Discernment, harmony and balance help you overcome self-defeating thoughts and emotions that have kept you from growing. Disempowering ideas and feelings are eliminated as your optimistic perspective and self-image are filled with empowering insights that assist you in balancing your life. Discouraging thoughts and feelings can now be discarded and replaced with more beneficial, healthy, and courageous ones. Courageous thoughts and feelings help you rise above discouraging thoughts and beliefs. The way to overcome resistances to growth and change is to develop an optimistic self-image.

• Your Optimistic Self-Image

Your optimistic self-image changes the way you picture yourself and creates new opportunities for you. Changing your perspective about who you are, and what you can and will do, creates new options and choices for living your life in an enthusiastic way. Understanding and developing the characteristics of an optimistic self-image such as confidence, courage, assertiveness, task-directedness, purpose, optimism, creativity, and effective communication will help you overcome self-defeating, self-sabotaging thoughts and emotions.

Confidence is the ability to make a change when you decide that your previous beliefs and emotions no longer bring you health and happiness. You have a strong identity and know what you're capable of becoming. Not being bound by the expectations of others, you operate as a free being capable of influencing your life's course. You know what you want. You are self-determining, independent, and free to feel, think, and act in a way that creates unlimited opportunities. You are a catalyst, stimulating and energizing yourself and others.

Courage is the willingness to act even without guarantees. You are able to take a stand because you willingly recognize and accept your empowering beliefs and actions. You are open to challenge. Rather than settling for less, you extend yourself to become more. You focus on change, effort, and self-worth. When you activate your awareness and sustain your beliefs, you become self-confident and develop self-respect.

Assertiveness means you are not timid or aggressive. You have earned what is rightfully yours, and what you deserve. You are able to stand on your own, continuously searching to find answers within yourself and with others. You are constantly improving the quality of life for yourself and others.

Task-directed means you focus on completing a task rather than focusing on your ego (self-gain). Task-directed means "we" are working together as a cohesive team, not "I" alone for my own benefit. Task-direction means that you make choices that impact your life and the lives of others. Your rewards (i.e., financial, emotional, physical, mental, spiritual) flow from successful completion of your work. When you set your direction and communicate to others about it, you are at the helm while allowing others to understand your thoughts, feelings and actions. The messages you send determine the messages you receive. Make them clear! Your mutual interaction and communication will ultimately determine your success.

Purpose is when you have clearly identifiable goals, and you understand your path and direction in life. The more detailed your goal, the clearer your plan. Knowing what you need determines the direction you will take to accomplish your goal. Becoming conscious and more aware of your actions and feelings will help to create inner strength and purpose, for yourself and others. When you have purpose, your actions are based on developing concern, respect, and trust for others. Ultimately, you value and believe that creating short and long-term personal and professional success for yourself, and others, creates a "collective confidence" to achieve incredible results in life.

Optimism means you are a winner, developing high self-esteem and self-confidence. Value your intuition and realize that it has unlimited power. When you decide to make positive choices, your optimism grows. Right turns become second nature and automatic. When you are optimistic, you become determined to find all the necessary means for self-realization. You then see problems as having solutions. Optimism helps you change negative emotions into positive ones, creating energy and mustering your inner resources to change your habitual, self-sabotaging behaviors. When you change your behaviors and emotions in an optimistic way, you realize that you're anchoring yourself to excitement, enthusiasm, and an abundant life filled with personal joy and well-being.

Creativity means you develop your own personal philosophy, or lifestyle, as an outgrowth of life experiences. You make your own decisions, and refuse to remain a victim of unproductive, earlier ones. You continually evaluate yourself, not being restrained by limiting self-definitions. And you give energy, power, and love to the positive choices and decisions that you make.

As an *Effective Communicator,* realize that you determine your behavior and communication. Don't isolate yourself from others. Your motivation to give, care, help, and empathize is born out of your own sense of self-worth and strength. Now imagine looking in a mirror and seeing your entire body, from head to toe. Visualize yourself in the mirror. You can change any part of your image. As your old image fades, the new image becomes brighter and clearer. Changing those parts of yourself that need modification changes your inner and outer-image. This also changes the way you view life. Changes in your physical, mental, emotional and spiritual *"self"* reflect your positive self-image pulsating with excitement. When you become optimistic— a winner—look and feel like a winner. A small change can make a world of difference!

Take this opportunity and make a commitment to change your image. What are some of the characteristics from your past identity (previous self-image) that you want to change? Use some of the characteristics mentioned above to help you change your image. Instead of procrastinating become more active, spontaneous, and cour-ageous. Use action words to describe your changes. You can also change your outer-image appearance (e.g., hairstyle, color of clothing, voice tempo and tone, positive nonverbal body language, congruent behaviors, etc.) to become more dynamic and high-spirited. Compose your list.

Past Identity ✦ ✦ ✦ ✦ ✦ ✦ ✦ ✦	Present/Future Identity
Plain clothes	In Vogue, up-to-date
Hair unkempt (no style)	Sharper Image, well-groomed
Procrastinator low inner-image (self-disesteem)	Action-oriented/decision-maker high inner-image (self-esteem)
Disinterested	Committed to excellence
_____	_____
_____	_____
_____	_____
_____	_____

Energize your assets and inner courage to accept life's challenges. Your new, vibrant way of looking, acting, feeling and thinking changes your self-image. As you begin to feel more awake and alive, your beliefs and feelings change. Your thoughts become more positive. Your feelings become uplifted when you take positive action. This will condition you for personal success. Changing your beliefs and feelings motivates you to take positive action toward reaching your goals.

A disempowering belief such as a self-defeating fiction creates a barrier to success and personal growth. An example of a self-defeating fiction that you need to overcome is, "Only superintelligent people become successful in life. There's no use in trying." You have now learned how to overcome your self-defeating beliefs and feelings by directing your feelings, behaviors, thoughts, and your communication in positive ways. When your attitude toward yourself, and others, remains open and attentive to new experiences, you are able to perceive reality in an accurate way.

Take the *I Can I Will* challenge! Overcome your fear by removing the barriers of self-defeating fictions and negative self-talk once and for all. Become a self-determining person, continually managing your emotions, beliefs, and behaviors while increasing your inner strength and freedom to experience life's abundance. Creating optimistic affirmations and positive self-statements depends on you! Your direction and attitude only become fixed when you stop making positive changes in your life. Imagine meeting yourself walking down the road.

When you enter into a discussion with yourself would you admire your accomplishments? Self-evaluation is essential for personal growth. Looking at yourself or someone else is like gazing into a multi-faceted gem. One must explore each facet to learn and appreciate the beauty of one's inner and outer image. Keep moving forward and constantly improve the quality of your life!

As an effective communicator, when you make positive changes you replace your self-defeating fictions with more beneficial, optimistic, and courageous beliefs. Now "will" yourself to overcome self-defeating fictions that have kept you from accomplishing your goals. Write your affirmations below.

Example: "I have the capability and intelligence to become optimistic and successful in the area (e.g., teaching, scuba diving, plumbing, carpentry, tennis, writing, dancing, singing, etc.) on which I choose to focus."

_____

_____

_____

Changing your beliefs and feelings motivates you to take positive action toward maximizing your enjoyment while reaching your goals.

The closer you get to your destination,
the more optimistic you become.

Now describe the new, optimistic you!

_____

_____

_____

Starting today, make your life clearer and brighter. Will it into being! Remember, when you commit or "will" yourself to do your best in whatever you're engaged in you summon your inner power. As you replace your self-defeating thoughts and actions with more courageous, optimistic ones you start to live life in an impeccable way. Empower yourself now and become one with your "will."

Choice pondered, "Your attitude, like your *'will,'* is similar to an inner compass." Choice knew that both he and Decision Making were standing on the crossroads.

Choice continued, "Then it's your *'attitude'* and *'will'* that provide you with the direction to help you find the balance between your thoughts, emotions and behaviors."

Decision Making replied, "Your *'attitude'* and *'will'* help you make the necessary changes in your life and tell you which way to go."

Decision Making was standing between the sun and the moon as the first rays of light etched across the purple sky.

Once again Decision Making responded, "Your optimistic, courageous action will direct you to find the right balance between your thoughts, feelings, and behaviors. You'll know which way to go and what to do when you get there."

Your actions are dictated by your inner map, your inner sense of 'self' or 'will'. This map is a combination of instinct and intellect that guides you toward your destination. You expand your psychological and emotional map when you make changes and empower yourself to move forward on the road to success. When you have choices and options your potential to grow and change is limitless. Having choices also enhances your inner strength and 'will'. As you build your self-esteem and hone your decision-making capabilities, your capacity to make positive choices skyrockets.

When you make positive decisions, you overcome self-defeating, self-sabotaging beliefs that once limited you. Empower yourself by creating a limitless well of health and vitality. Fill your well, your vessel, with positive choices!

Begin by formulating at least three alternatives to every situation. Stop looking at the same walls and doing the same thing everyday!

- *Make a decision to change the scenery, the environment or the schedule!* It's your choice!
- *Recognize and accept your own power.* Taking action, and experiencing life from a different perspective, creates a healthier and more optimistic attitude. Change your routines. When you watch a sunset as you drive along the ocean, stop the car, get out and

appreciate the moment. Climbing a mountain, exercising, painting, eating healthy food, listening to up-beat music, playing a team sport, taking photos or educational classes, whale watching, having a stimulating discussion, breathing clean air, drinking clean water, and any other positive experience, are just a few ways to expand your horizons. New situations, people, and new places that are nurturing will help you become more optimistic. Expand your attitude and self-image! Determine your own success!

- *Respect and appreciate yourself.* You can change by creating new experiences and resources in your life. Participate in relationships that offer opportunities for positive growth and change. Develop successful communication with others and create friendships that provide warmth, understanding, and unconditional acceptance. What are some new experiences and resources that you can develop for yourself? Take a moment to write them down.

New, positive experiences, persons, and resources help you create an encouraging and optimistic outlook. Challenge yourself to stay on track. Your optimistic perspective will assist you to take risks. It will also prepare you to think about making the necessary changes in your life. *Create a new focus!* Instead of investing energy in defensive behavior designed to block out new experiences, focus on developing yourself and your new ideas. New people, new places, and positive beliefs can reenergize your ideas and your self-image.

You might ask, "Why change my direction in life? What's wrong with the old picture, the same route?" Maybe nothing's wrong, and you are comfortable, secure, and stable in your life. If you feel comfortable at your present destination and the thought of change, redirection, or improving the quality of your life makes you feel anxious or uncomfortable then only use the information within this book to highlight your resources. I'm inviting you to take a look at your options. The decision to change may be for the sake of challenge which we all need. If you feel your comfort level outweighs your anxiety in your present situation, staying focused on actions that only increase your comfort may not encourage growth.

When you are discouraged because you are used to making so many wrong turns that the right ones don't seem to be an option anymore, then it's time to call on your inner courage and 'will' to help you make the change. Moving forward on the road to success means using your instincts and insights and developing your inner courage as the *"driving force"* to help you meet your anxiety and discomfort head-on. Experiencing some discomfort can motivate you to make changes you never thought were possible.

Empowering your way to success means that you have control over your own direction and your own path in life.

When you're alert, centered, and disciplined, inner movement and change is immediately registered. You're in control of your direction and destination. Becoming centered, or being grounded in yourself, is the highest state you can achieve. Achieving inner balance allows you to use your intelligence more fully. You are able to solve problems faster and more efficiently.

Achieving and maintaining optimal health, then, is a combination of developing positive beliefs, expectations, and behaviors.

Taking action to achieve your goals increases your self-esteem and optimism. Instead of developing unhealthy habits that block your growth, your mission is to put challenge, enthusiasm, and creativity back in your life.

Overcoming resistance takes courage. It also requires perseverance, self-discipline and optimism. Creating your own beliefs and expectations and choosing to act in responsible ways determine your destination. You are fully responsible for either setting yourself in motion or holding yourself back. You are also responsible for your actions, and the effect your actions have on others. When you take responsibility for your actions, you develop more self-respect and respect from others.

Self-respect, and respect for others, creates an enthusiasm and an energy that propel you forward. You are now conscientiously moving on the road to success developing agility and momentum as you become a whole, complete person. In the words of Henry David Thoreau, "If one advances confidently in the direction of his dreams, and endeavors to live the life which he has imagined, he will meet with success unexpected in common hours." Move with confidence and turn the wheel as you drive yourself in the direction of your dreams.

Influencing your own destiny, and taking charge of your self-esteem, leads you to greater self-acceptance and self-knowledge. When you believe you're in control of your life, you become alert to new opportunities.

The Journey is More Important Than The Destination

Whether you're traveling by land, sea or air, how many times have you heard someone say to you: "When are we going to get there?"; "can't we go any faster?"; "what's taking so long?" Some people believe that the destination is more important than the journey, minimizing the importance of the journey. Enjoying the sights and sounds, the thoughts and ideas, and simple moments before you get "there," can be just as rewarding.

Your involvement in certain personal and professional relationships is similar to taking a journey. How can you truly understand anyone if you're always rushing to interpret what they're going to say or do? Hasty interpretations, or interjecting your own attitude into the situation, can create biased perceptions. "Seeing" things from your own point of view, without really checking out the situation, can color your interpretations.

How many times do you have to make the wrong turn before you decide to make the right one? Changing your route, or detouring, can have a positive outcome. You can turn an unproductive relationship, or situation, into one that promises more productivity and happiness. First, *understand* the perceptions of others as well as your own; second, *adjust or correct* your perceptions and communication as needed; third, *choose* to move on with the relationship; or fourth, *make a decision* to change direction altogether and start over again if working on reaching your goals is unfulfilling. Taking action and learning how to adjust and change are part of your journey. Understand and appreciate your resources and perceptions.

Your freedom to make *wise choices, sound decisions* and *congruent changes* are the most important elements in any situation. Your new identity and heightened self-esteem increase your capacity to take responsibility for your own development, This will assist you in developing the courage to charge ahead toward achieving your goals.

Know when it's time to stay on your road or change direction. Remember, it's your belief about the destination that ultimately creates its importance. And you are in control of your beliefs! One purpose of your journey is to become more self-aware, to freely experience all aspects of your changing, evolving self. As you liberate yourself, and shed your past skin, you become more optimistic. An optimistic attitude will bring out your personal strengths and insights, powerfully enhancing your life along the way. When you feel empowered, you can empower others as well. As a result, your relationships and communication become more fulfilling and productive. *Charge yourself with enthusiasm for building a dynamic future!*

There's no need to spend time and energy making excuses. When you focus your insights and actions on achieving your goals and dreams, your roadblocks will diminish. *Empower yourself and become aware of your positive actions and choices!*

When you take the time to communicate with and smile at others on the way toward your destination, you turn liabilities into assets. Begin now and become more constructive in your relationships. Turn your new insights into power that propels you toward success

Create Your Own Positive, Personal Journey!

Making healthy contact and connecting with people are just as important as getting to the destination. When others believe you are interested in them, they become more interested in what you say and do. Show them that you're sincerely committed to open and honest communication, and you'll experience an unlimited energy and enthusiasm in their expressiveness and productivity.

Positively changing your thoughts, feelings and behaviors *can* and *will* condition you for success. As Joseph McVinney used to say, "Wake Up and Smell the Coffee!"

Whether it's becoming the best person you can become, personally and professionally, or the most sincere friend, spouse, or parent, in your personal relationships, *appreciating the journey is more important than the destination.*

Become *understanding and conscientious!* Think about which

direction you need to go and what you have to do to make the most out of your relationships with others. Creating healthy outcomes in your relationships is a main ingredient for success.

When you become understanding and conscientious, you assume control of your mental and physical skills to achieve peak performance. You can now take charge of your own personal power. You have ultimate control of your own beliefs, actions, and experiences. When you take charge of all your inner and outer resources, you give yourself permission for higher achievement. You create your own choices! You possess an incredible gift: *The strength to develop your "will" and become successful!*

Self-Discipline and Focus

Søren Kierkegaard wrote, "To venture causes anxiety, but not to venture is to lose one's self . . . and to venture in the highest sense is precisely to become conscious of one's self." Becoming more conscious of your 'self' and assuming responsibility for your success requires *self-discipline and focus.* Meeting, and exceeding, your expectations and creating a new, optimistic self-image depends on you! When you want to be successful, you have to *'choose your own attitude.'* Harvey Mackay (1990) writes, "With champions, success lies in the journey, not the destination. With champions, success is never unexpected; it's a result that comes from continuous, unselfish, unrelenting determination to win, never letting down, never letting outside influences into the game. Champions know it's not having the talent to win that makes a champion; it's having too much pride to lose. Season after season. Year after year. Championship after championship. Lombardi's team never lost. Occasionally, they just ran out of time" (p. 358).

Changing yourself means making the commitment to overcome any resistance. This means motivating yourself by creating positive energy towards competitive and challenging situations. Stop cluttering yourself with doubts and countless little nagging thoughts directed towards failure. Become determined to succeed and concentrate all conscious effort, both physical and mental, towards achieving your goals. Overcoming resistance takes concentration and determination. You have to *commit* yourself and truly *believe* that you have the *"will"* to win!

Choosing the road to success depends on your continuous, unrelent-

ing determination to take positive action to achieve your goals. You will succeed when you have perseverance and purpose. Developing your own inner strength and self-esteem means that you must become self-responsible, self-deciding, and self-determining. You can accomplish most anything; whether or not you will is a decision only you can make. When you accept yourself and make the commitment to move forward, you will meet with success. Accept it with your whole heart and mind.

You must now shed the shackles of your past experiences and transform yourself. Shedding the shackles that have kept you from growing and overcoming resistance requires discipline. "This discipline is not just an athletic ability mastered through physical practice alone, it is a skill with its origin in mental exercise" (Herrigel, 1971). When the archer hits the mental and physical center of his inner self, he has established a center point of reference to himself. Yet, to check his own center, he must split the preceeding arrow with another, to see that he is consistently on the same center, the same mark.

Target Yourself for Success!

When you feel more capable and responsible, you become more capable and responsible as you move toward self-fulfillment. Allow yourself the freedom to become centered in consciousness. And when you arrive at the crossroads, you will remain centered. *A centered person is always on the crossroads, always on the same mark, where Choice and Decision Making become one.*

The lightning charged the sky as Choice and Decision Making arrived at the top of the mountain. Choice gazed at the distant desert plain when he turned and asked Decision Making, "What is the direction now—The Grand Finale? What seeds of awareness can we plant? What pearls of wisdom can we share as we walk the path of truth? What is the last word?!"

Decision Making replied, "When seeking truth, we must first formulate the question. One must be centered and balanced on the crossroads of life. You cannot fool yourself. You can only go forward, not backwards. However, you need to watch where you're going while you increase your own awareness. Don't step on anything that's defenseless. Move with positive motion empowering those with whom you come into contact."

Decision Making pointed to a double-arc rainbow that the sun and rain had created when he said, "You can *'choose'* your own attitude and *'decide'* your own destination!''

Pave your road to success with perseverance, courage and determination. Venture forth and make your own decisions. It's your choice. Choosing your own way is to live life fully and actively shape the events in your life. When you freely express yourself, you become more alive, decisive and optimistic. Your optimism will help you develop positive relationships with others. Your optimism, combined with your perseverance, courage and determination, will catapult you toward your goals. Your self-worth will soar as you willingly and courageously sprint forward on your road to success.

In the highest sense, *when you want to move and take action, you need to turn your inner key.* Your inner key is your *"inner will"* which guides and encourages you throughout your life. Your "inner will" is the force that increases and charges your self-confidence and physical capabilities and gives you the momentum and determination to move forward.

When you take responsibility for who you are and the actions you take, you motivate yourself to become renewed each and every day. Believe you have a future and live every day with passion!

Remember: I Can I Will!

References

Buber, Martin. *I and Thou.* New York: Charles Scribner's Sons, 1970.

Castaneda, Carlos. *Tales of Power.* New York: Simon and Schuster, 1974.

Davis Jr., Sammy. *Yes I Can.* New York: Farrar, Straus and Giroux, 1965.

Dinkmeyer, D., & L. Losoncy. *The Encouragement Book.* New York: Prentice Hall Press, 1980.

Dyer, Dr. Wayne W. *You'll See It When You Believe IT.* New York: William Morrow and Company, Inc., 1989.

Ellis, A. *Humanistic Psychotherapy.* New York: McGraw-Hill, 1973.

Garfield, Charles A. *Peak Performance.* New York: Warner Books, 1984.

Gibran, Kahlil. *The Prophet.* New York: Alfred A. Knopf, 1969.

Herrigel, Eugen. *Zen in the Art of Archery.* New York: Vintage Books, 1971.

Hesse, Hermann. *Siddhartha.* New York: A New Directions Book. 1951.

_____. *Narcissus and Goldmund.* New York: Farrar, Straus and Giroux, 1968.

_____. *Demian.* New York: Bantam Books, 1970.

Hill, Napoleon. *Think and Grow Rich.* New York: Fawcett Crest, 1969.

Krishnamurti, J. *The First and Last Freedom.* New York: Harper, 1954.

Losoncy, Lewis E. *Turning People On.* New York: Prentice Hall Press, 1977.

Losoncy, Lewis E. *You Can Do It.* New York: Prentice Hall Press, 1980.

Mackay, Harvey. *Beware The Naked Man Who Offers You His Shirt.* New York: Ballantine Books, 1991.

_____. *Swim with Sharks Without Being Eaten Alive.* New York: Ballantine Books, 1989.

Maltz, Maxwell. *Psycho-Cybernetics.* Beverly Hills, CA: Wilshire Books, 1960.

May, Rollo. *Love and Will.* New York: Norton, 1969.

Perls, Frederick S. *Gestalt Therapy Verbatim.* Moab, Utah: The Real People Press, 1969.

Rogers, Carl. *On Becoming a Person.* Boston: Houghton-Mifflin, 1961.

——— . *Person to Person.* California: Real People Press, 1967.

Thoreau, Henry David. *Walden.* New York: Modern Library, 1937.

Zastrow, C. *Talk to Yourself.* Englewood Cliffs, N.J.: Prentice-Hall, 1979.

Organizational Designs in Communication

Organizational Designs in Communication (ODC) is a consulting firm of professionals. ODC was formed in 1985 to provide a quality training partnership with business and organizations. It is ODC's intent to improve the quality of the work environment, products, and services.

ODC offers a full range of programs conducted by professionals who include consultants in senior management and teaching faculty members from education, manufacturing, research, health care, human resources, retail, communications, sales and marketing.

A brief list of our recent clients includes Xerox, Cox Cable, The Catholic Archdiocese of Los Angeles, the State of California Department of Personnel Administration, and San Diego Community College District.

Our vision is to provide *Continual Quality Improvement through Focused Commitment*. This statement simply means that we are concerned with developing ongoing programs that provide people and organizations with tools necessary to improve the quality of everyday organizational life. This then can be translated into improved productivity, customer service, and ultimately increased profits and market share. Self-motivated employees working within a positive environment produce positive results.

At ODC it is our mission to provide organizations with training and support of Total Quality Programs. It is our intent to work with clients to introduce, develop, and maintain Organizational Development and Total Quality Programs within our client base.

Results You Can Expect

Improved Organizational Climate, Improved Motivation, Improved Teamwork, Expanded Communication Channels, Increased Productivity, Individual Improvement

Training Workshops and Action Programs

I Can I Will™ Seminars, Total Quality Management Programs, Relationship Awareness Training™, Developing Leadership Skills for Supervisors, Interpersonal Communication to Improve Organizational Effectiveness, Managing Stress and Conflict, Train the Trainer, The Power of Positive Influence, Developing High Performance Teams, Positive People Skills, Motivating Yourself & Others, Training in Developing & Maintaining Effective Communication, Management Leadership Institute.

Dr. Frederick Elias is an internationally recognized lecturer, educator, and consultant of human resource and organizational development. An expert in communications and motivation, Dr. Elias designs, implements, and conducts leadership training, team building, communication, staff development, and productivity improvement programs.

Organizational Designs in Communication
Post Office Box 60609 • Santa Barbara, California 93160 • (805) 968-1666

For limited edition prints of the illustrations in this book, write to
Gordon Phelps, Post Office Box 154, Mt. Laguna, California 91948